The Antique
Story Book

For Christine —
With best wishes —

The Antique Story Book

Finding the Real Value of Old Things

Enjoy !

Arthur Schwerdt

iUniverse, Inc.

New York Lincoln Shanghai

The Antique Story Book
Finding the Real Value of Old Things

iUniverse books may be ordered through booksellers or by contacting:

iUniverse
2021 Pine Lake Road, Suite 100
Lincoln, NE 68512
www.iuniverse.com
1-800-Authors (1-800-288-4677)

Because of the dynamic nature of the Internet, any Web addresses or links contained in this book may have changed since publication and may no longer be valid.

The views expressed in this work are solely those of the author and do not necessarily reflect the views of the publisher, and the publisher hereby disclaims any responsibility for them.

ISBN: 978-0-595-42479-5 (pbk)
ISBN: 978-0-595-86814-8 (ebk)

Printed in the United States of America

Contents

Part III   *Stories About Ceramics*

Part IV   *Stories About Glass*

Part V   *Stories About Metals And Jewelry*

Part VI   Stories About Books And Prints

Part VII   Stories About Collectibles

Acknowledgments

No one writes a newspaper column for over two decades without having some wonderful people to thank.

First of all there is my friend, Joe Zelnik, long time editor of the *Cape May County Herald,* who believed in my column from the beginning and still publishes it to this day. Thanks, too, to Joan Nash and Carolyn Mee at that paper.

Special thanks to another friend, Joe Daly, my editor at the good old *Atlantic City Sun* and, later, at the *Sandpaper* in Ocean City, who encouraged me to make my column more literary, alive and personal.

Thanks, too, to my friend, Steve Wheaton, who loves to tell stories and let me use a couple of them here.

I am very grateful for the help and encouragement of a very good old friend, Charles Frary, without whose exceptional editorial skills, this book would be a mess. Any errors that still remain are all mine.

And then there is the brilliantly creative Larry Damato, who continues to inspire me after more than three decades, and to whom this book is affectionately dedicated.

Introduction
It's All About The Stories

My friend, Steve, a fellow antique dealer, once showed me a familiar pair of old wire rim sunglasses that he said he was going to offer for sale in his shop. He wanted my opinion on what to charge for them, but asked that I first read the printed card he planned to display with them.

It told this story:

"These sunglasses were given to me by an old friend, a retired U. S. naval officer, who told me he had received them from another naval officer during World War II, while both were recuperating at a military hospital in the South Pacific. My friend had been there for about two weeks, when he was finally taken outside in a wheelchair for a breath of fresh air. Having been inside so long, he was momentarily blinded by the midday sun as he passed through the door.

"When he put up his hand to shield his eyes, he heard a voice say, 'Here, sailor, put these on,' and was handed a pair of sunglasses. He was whisked away before he could say thank you, but vowed to find the person who gave him the glasses and return them.

"After a day or two asking around, he finally found the officer who had given him the sunglasses, but the fellow wouldn't take them back. He said they were not his, but had been given to him not long after he had arrived at the hospital by Gen. Douglas MacArthur, who had been visiting the troops there. MacArthur had told him that he had received the glasses on a fishing trip. When his own sunglasses had fallen over-board, his fishing companion, Ernest Hemingway, had offered him his pair.

"Astonished at this story, my friend asked the officer his name. It was John F. Kennedy."

There on the bottom of the card were three photographs, one each of Hemingway, MacArthur and Kennedy, each wearing sunglasses identical to the pair Steve was showing me.

"Now," said Steve, "turn the card over."

On the back, printed in bold block letters, the card read: "IF YOU BELIEVE THIS STORY, YOU SHOULD NOT BE OUT ANTIQUING."

It was something of a cruel joke, but Steve had made his point. When it comes to celebrity cachet, people, especially Americans, can be very gullible, even when they're out looking for antiques.

I've seen this so many times at auctions, where people have paid exorbitant prices for the most banal household and personal items just because they may have been used once by some famous person.

For those who understand and enjoy antiques, however, the stories that really matter are those that tell about the times and places these things were made, who made them and how and why. These are the stories that make antiques come alive again to do what they do best—truly evoke their times for us. Through them we learn that nothing we see on antique shop shelves was created in a vacuum. They were created by real people who, like us, are each a part of a moment in history—its literature, music, art, commerce, politics, technology, domestic life and economics.

You might say that the lure of antiques is the lore of antiques. When you learn that lore, antique shops are no longer just collections of silent stuff, but become filled with the chatter of history. The truth is you can buy a vase in any department store, but when you buy it in an antique shop, it comes with a story. It's the story that makes it so valuable and makes antiquing so much more meaningful and enjoyable.

If you enjoy a good story like the ones in this collection, you have an instinct for seeing the real value of old things, and you definitely should be out antiquing.

PART I
Stories About Periods
And Styles

Love And Sex Victorian Style * The Edwardians—When Men Were Men * Another Time For Melisande * At Home With Pappa Biedermeier * Funny Furniture Names * In Old Vienna * These Three Kings * The Secrets Of Eastlake's Success * Art Deco—The Past As Future * For Comfort, It's Wicker, Naturally * An American Original * It's All Done With Mirrors * Through The Gargoyle's Eye

Love And Sex—Victorian Style

Antiquing is very much like a form of archeology. Historians may be able to tell you a great deal about a past society's politics and economics, but we can dig up even more intimate details about the past just by foraging in flea markets, yard sales and antique shops.

Antique hunters are forever unearthing evidence of how people prepared food and dined, how they dressed, entertained themselves, decorated their homes and even what their attitudes were toward love and sex.

The Victorian courting bench and courting lamp, for instance, reveal a society where the courtship between a young man and woman was extremely formal, public, ritualized, and very much controlled by the parents.

A courting bench is an S-shaped chair, where two people sit straight up and face-to-face. Because of its configuration, the chair can't be hidden in a corner or stuck against a wall. It has to float in a room, visible from all sides.

The occupants of a courting bench might be close together, but there's certainly no room for scrunching down and smooching. This kind of chair is also known by one of two French terms: a "*tête-à-tête*" (head to head) or a "*causeuse*" (conversation bench) from the word "*causer*" (to chat), from a time when courting was more about talking than necking.

Accompanying the courting bench was a courting lamp—a small device consisting of a base of wood, marble or alabaster supporting a decorative brass rod, curved at the top to support a glass receptacle just big enough to hold a small votive-style candle. The young lady's father lit the candle at the beginning of her suitor's visit, and when the candle went out it was time for the young man to say good-night.

Victorian courtship may have been formal and proper, but remember that in most dictionaries, the second meaning of the adjective Victorian might be listed as "pertaining to the moral standards of the age, especially when stuffy and hypocritical" (Webster Collegiate).

Victorian courtship may have been about talking, but some things just never got talked about, and sex was one of them. Antique hunters are finding the answer to how young Victorians got information about sex and marriage. It's in those slim little how-to pamphlets once advertised in newspapers or available from clergymen and physicians, who would rather hand you a book than talk about such things face-to-face.

These pamphlets had alluring titles like: "The Relations of the Sexes," "How To Make Love," "Facts for Wives," "Sexual Physiology Revealed," and, pompously, "The Reproductive Element in Man, as a Means to His Elevation and Happiness."

The authors, mostly doctors, but often just *soi-disant* experts and almost always men, mixed current lore, superstition and some science in a lofty, circumloquacious prose. They sometimes sounded even a bit apologetic for talking about such things, and rarely talked about "the act" at all, except in the most coldly scientific terms.

Advice was often conflicting. In one manual, women are told to refrain from too lusty an enjoyment of sexual pleasure lest the offspring of such a union be defiled by the spirit of such lust. In another volume, the author attributes many of women's ills and depressions to their failure to take enjoyment in the sexual act.

In the days before condoms, women were encouraged by some pamphleteers to go horseback riding or dancing the day after intercourse so as to prevent conception. Yet another expert warns against such a practice as not only ineffective, but likely to result in monstrous conceptions.

Despite the conflicting advice, these books were always written with an air of absolute authority. Many of them were published over and over again, right through the turn of the century, without regard for any advances in social or scientific theory.

All of these manuals, however, make fascinating reading and are a real insight into the Victorian mind. Some of them actually give sound advice about the importance of love and companionship, important things to consider in a world where divorce was unthinkable.

Much Victorian style was based on a revival of the Gothic and Renaissance styles, and this is reflected in the grand Victorian wedding.

The traditional Victorian wedding is a staged medieval fairy tale. The young maiden princess, worshiped from afar, descends down the aisle dressed in virginal white to be presented by her father (who has been in control since those courting days) to the prince charming of her dreams.

Antique-shop archeologists can usually find authentic pieces of these ceremonies—old Victorian lace, veils and entire wedding dresses, toasting goblets, wedding cake servers, wedding albums, sterling nosegay holders, crystal flower baskets, etc.

Of course, in a society as hypocritical as the Victorians', love and sex had a backroom, too. In fact, most of the erotica on today's antiques market is from the Victorian age. Collectors of such things have discovered pornographic literature and devices that certainly could have scared the horses. But there is also a wealth of more "innocent" erotica, like naughty novelties, bawdy figurines, nude and erotic postcards and prints.

More than merely a titillating peek into the private lives of an age long ago, uncovering the relics of love and sex in the Victorian era has got to leave us with at least one haunting, and perhaps sobering, thought. There will be antique hunters in the next century. What will they find out about us?

The Edwardians—When Men
Were Men

In the late 19th Century the New England poet, James Russell Lowell, wrote, "Yea, Manhood hath a wider span/And larger privilege of life than man."

Lowell's lines are at the center of what was one of the most important and far-reaching discussions of his day—What is manliness?

His answer has repercussions even to this day—Manhood is an ideal for which each man must strive, and against which each man must judge himself.

If today's women sometimes wonder why men are such jerks, and if men find themselves wondering how they could be such jerks, both might well find the answer in the development of the 19th Century "Ideal of Manliness," which culminated in the turn-of-the-century "Age of Men," those halcyon days just before the women got the vote.

Since the sexual revolution of the 1960s, it seems that gender identity, whether it's Gay Rights or the Women's Movement, is all we can talk about. It's a main topic on the TV talk-show circuit and a primary theme for TV sitcoms. (The old show called "Men Behaving Badly" isn't too obvious, is it?) And not long ago, one of the longest running best-sellers on the N.Y Times list (190 weeks) was John Gray's "Men Are From Mars, Women Are From Venus."

As women try to define their role in today's society, the idea of manliness and virility they have to deal with has its roots in what we might call "Victorian Macho." While it might be a cliche to say, "In the good old days, when men were men," that is exactly where the Victorian ideals of Manhood were coming from.

The good old days for Victorian men were the Middle Ages, and the romantic ideal was the knight, a man among men who went out into the world and fought the good fight while the damsels stayed home knitting tapestries.

The golden age for Victorian Macho came in the turn-of-the-century Edwardian era (1890-1915), when the carousing Prince Eddy was on the throne of England (1901-1910) and bully-bully Teddy Roosevelt was in the American White House (1901-1909).

Here's an interesting insight into Theodore Roosevelt. A sickly rich boy with an Ivy League education, he lost his first election to the New York State Assembly after being accused by the opposition of being a "Jane Dandy" and "an Oscar Wilde."

Chastened by the Victorian ideal of virility, he transformed himself into a bear-hunting, rough-riding, San Juan Hill-charging, Panama Canal-building man's man, who would eventually see "war as the ideal condition of human society, for the manly strenuousness which it involves."

The Roosevelt/Edwardian era, however, is not called the "Age of Men" only because of how men influenced politics and world affairs. It is also a time when masculine tastes would have a strong influence on art and architecture, and particularly on decorative design.

Prince Eddy, who was said to have affected the trilled "r" of a manly Scottish burr, once proclaimed, "I don't know much about arrrrt, but I do know something about decorrrrating."

The turn-of-the-century antiques we see on today's market were not created in a vacuum. They are a product of their times, and the best of them will make those times come alive for us again.

For this pre-World War I period, that means a celebration of manly pursuits, especially hunting.

Sharp-eyed antiquers will find hunting and fishing motifs from this period, including game and safari animals, on items as varied as table china, vases, inkwells, wall sconces, figurines, furniture, lamps, chandeliers, and more.

Since the manly ideal required the man to work outside the home and bring home the bounty, we should also notice how many materials from the outdoors came indoors at this time.

Turn-of-the-century decorative objects, utilitarian items like table and vanity accessories, and even jewelry and other items of personal fashion were made of or decorated with mother-of-pearl, ivory, amber, coral, pearl, feathers, bone, horn, tortoise shell, animal fur, and leather.

Edwardian antiques are also replete with nautical motifs including sailing ships, billowing waves, anchors, ropes, various sea creatures, especially dolphins, and that seagoing male's fantasy, the mermaid.

Another Time For Melisande

Some time ago, I sold a hand-painted porcelain plaque. It was marked on the back, "CFH," for Charles Field Haviland, and I dated it just prior to the turn of the century. The painting was an elaborate portrait in profile of the fictional character, Mélisande.

The artist's signature on the front was illegible, but it must have been the work of one of the earliest Art Nouveau artists, many of them anonymous, who worked in small communes in the European countryside, places very much like where this plaque was made, in Limoges, the principal city of the rural French province of Limousine.

These artists and other craftsmen had left the newly industrialized cities as part of what we now call the Arts and Crafts Movement. Initially, their work imitated nature, but as the movement matured they became bolder, and their work became more stylized. Instead of simply copying nature, they copied from nature—its organic movement and fluid, curving lines. In short, they discovered the essential femininity of Mother Nature, and this is what they celebrated.

It is a limping theory of mine that major changes in the cultural history of the world happen as a result of changes in our attitude toward women and women's attitude about themselves. Men may have made war and business and thus affected the political history of the globe, but women have always had the power to affect the cultural soul of mankind.

This, I think, is what the ancients were telling us: the Trojan War fought for Helen; Aeneas's destiny nearly thwarted by Dido; Ulysses' kingdom saved by Penelope.

The elevation of women in the Middle Ages governs the social (courtly love) and religious (the Cult of the Virgin) life of those times. And it is in the full flower of their humanity that the earthy Madonnas of the Renaissance define that age.

In somewhat the same way, Mélisande became the ideal representation for the turn of the century. You have seen her, although you may not have known it was her. She is the model for all those otherwise nameless female figures in the artwork and on the decorative accessories of the period. She is in stained glass windows, clocks and on theatrical posters; she holds up lamps and urns; she is carved on furniture and painted on vases and, of course, plaques.

Her face is serene, even aloof. She seems aristocratic, but she is also a free spirit, a child of nature. She may wear a crown, but her untamed hair flies out from under it. Her story, like all the really important ones, is a tragedy.

Those who are familiar with Mélisande know her from the opera, "Pelléas et Mélisande," by Claude Debussy. The opera debuted at the Opéra Comique in Paris on April 30, 1902, but it is based on a play written ten years earlier by Maurice Maeterlinck.

The story is set in an ancient kingdom called Allemonde, where the old man, Arkel, is king. He has two sons, Golaud, the eldest, and the youthful Pelléas.

One day Golaud is coming through the dense forest outside the kingdom and discovers a young maiden by the side of a pond. She is lost and confused; she does not know who she is, but feels she may be a princess and has somehow lost her crown in the depths of the pond. Because she is so beautiful, Golaud thinks she must be a princess and vows to care for her and protect her. He takes her back to the kingdom, gives her a ring, and marries her.

Not long afterwards, Mélisande is musing by a fountain when she meets Pelléas. It is a magical fountain, said to be able to open the eyes of the blind. Both Pelléas and Mélisande realize their eyes have been opened to the love they share for one another. Then, all of a sudden, as Mélisande fingers the fountain's waters, she loses her wedding ring.

Golaud, who has been wounded in a riding accident, notices the missing ring when Mélisande comes to his sick bed. He orders her to return to the fountain to find it, and tells Pelléas to accompany her. Through a spy (his son by a previous marriage), Golaud learns of the love between Pelléas and Mélisande and confronts her. He pulls her by the hair, but Arkel intervenes to keep him from killing her. Mélisande runs from Golaud to the fountain and again meets Pelléas. Golaud discovers them there and stabs his brother to death, whereupon Mélisande announces she is pregnant.

Mélisande gives birth (I think it is a daughter), forgives Golaud, confesses that the child is his and that her love for Pelléas was innocent. (Was it?) Then she dies.

As operas go, the action here is static. The lines are sung like straight dialogue without any big climaxes, arias or ensembles. The score is as amorphous as gas.

The story is relentlessly dreary. It is as murky as a dream, and just as thick with confounding symbolism. The characters are more shadows than real flesh and blood. Almost no one likes it. Those who do defend it as an important attempt to make opera audiences explore the psychology of the characters rather than simply react to them emotionally. But the psychology, with its Freudian pools of repressed sexuality, is dated and sophomoric.

So, how does Mélisande emerge from this quagmire as a symbol of her age? Because this time it is not a man, but a woman who is torn between love and duty. Like the new century, she is wedded to the old but needs the young. She is, as we all are, a child of nature, unaware of how we got here, weighed down by centuries of civilization not of our own making.

The death of Mélisande is a warning of what can happen if we insist on taking old baggage into a new century. It may be a reminder that if we want to take beauty and innocence with us, it is best we understand that we are not other than nature, but part of nature. And the playwright's way of reaffirming our faith in nature can surely be interpreted in Mélisande's ultimate delivery of a child, albeit on her deathbed.

Well, I know it is time for me to stop philosophizing when I start using words like "albeit." But I promised the lady who bought the portrait plate that I would some day explain the story of that hapless girl.

This is supposed to be the "Age of the Woman." As we start the 21st Century, Mélisande stands ready once again to be pressed into service as a symbol. In the coming years, how women will define themselves in the home, in society and in their personal relationships will undoubtedly play an important role in how this new millennium evolves.

At Home With Papa Biedermeier

Biedermeier is pronounced "BEE-der-my-er," and it's one of the most fascinating, important and sought-after furniture styles of the 19th Century. It is also the most misunderstood, mainly because we don't see much of it, especially in rural antique shops.

It doesn't help that there was never any place or person named Biedermeier and, not only is the name a total fiction, but it was not even used to describe the style until around 1900, well after the Biedermeier period was over. But more about the name later.

Understanding Biedermeier is made more complex because historians don't agree on dating this German/Austrian style. Some purists place "true" Biedermeier only between 1815 and 1830, with later versions of the style continuing until 1848. Others note that the style really did dominate the era from 1800 to 1880, especially in central Europe.

Descriptions of the style vary, too. The one you may hear most often is, "a German middle-class version of the French Empire," which is true to an extent. However, it is much more distinctive and innovative than that. Let's try to visualize it.

Biedermeier is a classical style, meaning it is balanced, linear and masculine. This is as opposed to the more feminine styles, like Rococo (Louis XV) and Art Nouveau, which tend to be more organic and curvilinear or serpentine.

As a classical style, Beidermeier was influenced by the English Adam and Hepplewhite styles and the French neo-classical styles like Louis XVI, Directoire and Empire. In turn, Biedermeier would influence 20th Century classical styles like German Bauhaus (1919) and French Art Deco (1925).

In fact, Biedermeier often looks so much like Art Deco that people confuse the two. But Biedermeier is warmer and homier than Deco or any of the other classical styles, which tend to be more cool and stately, even haughty.

It is the hominess of Biedermeier that inspired writers at the turn of the century to give the style its name.

The name comes from a satirical caricature, Papa (Gottlieb) Biedermeier (originally spelled, "Biedermaier"), who appeared in a weekly German language newspaper called *Fliegende Blatter* (Flying Leaves). Publisher, Ludwig Eichrodt, and his friend, Adolph Kussmaul, combined the names of two of the paper's previous satirical characters, Biedermann and Bummelmaier.

The caricature, Papa Biedermeier, was a satire of the comfortable German middle class, content to stay in their homes and enjoy the simple things of life. To understand why such a life would be the object of ridicule, it helps to know a bit about the politics of the time.

At the dawn of the 19th Century, the German-speaking people of central Europe were divided into many small, old feudal principalities. To defend against Napoleon, however, a single all-German army had been assembled. This fact, along with the successes of the American and French Revolutions, got some people, especially urban intellectuals, dreaming about establishing a united German republic.

This dream was nipped in the bud by the Austrian chancellor, Prince von Metternich ("Prince von Midnight" to his many detractors), who convened the Congress of Vienna in 1815 to protect the power of the local aristocracy.

The result was a brutal, if bumbling, regimen of curfews, censorship (even of the mails), surveillance and limits on travel. Any idea of revolution was finally out of the question when the middle class capitulated by retreating to their country homes and the comforts of blissful domesticity.

It was this complacency of the bourgeoisie that was satirized in the caricature of Papa Beidermeier. But the style wasn't named for him until around 1900 by critics finally weary of middle-class Victorian.

Middle-class domestic life is actually celebrated in the kinds of furniture you will find in the Biedermeier style.

There are game tables and worktables, elaborate sewing cabinets, bookcases, secretaries, writing cabinets and ladies' desks, all geared for everyday household activities. Showcases and etageres displayed family heirlooms and collections.

Although most of the forms were simple and geometric, and the decorations sparse, the artful veneers on most Beidermeier pieces reflect a charming warmth.

What was simple and homey 200 years ago has become elegant and expensive now. I wonder if they will be able to say the same about the way we live today two centuries in the future.

Funny Furniture Names

Let's play funny furniture names. You may have heard of them, but what are they? And where did they get those funny names?

Credenza

A credenza is a side cabinet. It is a bit more compact than a sideboard, but much fancier, in the Italian style or French style. The French sometimes call the piece a "commode dessert," a server for post-prandial sweets.

The credenza's shape is often rounded at the ends and there is sometimes a marble top. There are doors and drawers and occasionally there are open shelves down the sides. It will be heavily veneered, inlaid, painted with scenes or florals, or decorated with ormolu (gilt metal).

The word *"credenza"* is Italian for trust. During the Renaissance, food and wine was placed on the credenza to be tested by servants for poison. This way, one's guest could dine free from fear of assassination, except that they still would have to keep an eye on that lady with the tricky ring. (And we think politics is tough today.)

Credenze (that's technically the plural) were popular again during the Renaissance Revival of the late Victorian/Edwardian era at the turn of the century. Today they are not restricted to the dining room, but serve as great display pieces anywhere. A credenza can function wonderfully, for instance, as an elegant bar, where guest can choose their own poison. Trust me.

Bonheur-du-Jour

Speaking of happy hour, that's the literal meaning of *bonheur*, the French word for happiness. A bonheur-du-jour (happiness of the day) is a fancy lady's fancy desk. It is a narrow piece with tall legs, a drawer and a writing surface, sometimes concealed by a cylinder and sometimes hinged for storage underneath. There is a small bookcase or cabinet on top that may have mirrored doors.

This is where the lady of the house would write her daily correspondence—thank you notes, invitations, etc.—in the morning, aptly in the morning room. She would also assign tasks to the staff—shopping lists, menus, her wardrobe, etc.—which made her feel important and thus, apparently, very happy.

Recamier

What made Madame Récamier feel happy and important was to greet guests to her salon while reclining. In the late 1700s, she ordered her furniture maker to make a sofa with no back and scrolling arms on each side, which we now call after her—a recamier.

Mme Récamier looked so happy and important reclining on her recamier that the French artist, David, painted a now famous portrait of her posed on it.

Pembroke Table

About the same time, the English countess, Lady Pembroke, was not lying around. In England that would be considered very unladylike.

Instead, she was entertaining her guests at tea on the very practical table that bears her name.

The Pembroke table is a sofa table or end table with drop-leaves and a drawer. The tables would be displayed against a wall, or behind or on either side of a sofa, then taken out and opened up for tea parties.

Davenport

Another practical English invention is the Davenport desk. Originally listed in a 1790s catalogue of the Lancaster furniture maker, Gillows, as a "Captain Davenport," it is a narrow, heavy piece with its drawers on one side, a space-saving feature that's perfect for the small confines of a ship captain's cabin.

Confusion arises in 1833, however, when the piece is referred to as a "devenport" in John Loudon's "Encyclopedia of Cottage, Farm and Villa Architecture and Furniture," and listed as a "drawing room writing-cabinet for ladies," like the bonheur-du-jour.

Further confusion occurs in the late 19th century, when folks start referring to a kind of convertible sofa as a "davenport." How the sofa got its name is not clear, but it seems a good place to rest up from all the confusion.

Canterbury

The canterbury is a portable rack for sheet music. It would be easy to compare the canterbury to a magazine rack, since that's how so many of them are used today, but that would be misleading.

The canterbury, which first appeared around 1800 in the cathedral that gives it its name, is much more elaborate. Some are so strange looking, you may wonder what they are.

Usually square, at least at the base, and mounted on rolling casters, a canterbury will have a drawer or stretcher shelf at the bottom and open compartments on top for organizing the sheet music. Sometimes there will be a handle.

For Victorians, a canterbury was a must in the second parlor or music room. Furniture makers of the time showed off their skills making them—turned-wood spindles, classical x-frames, Gothic or Romanesque arches.

Commode

What exactly is a commode? The word comes from the same root as our word "accommodate"—to make suitable. Suitable for what depends on how you need to be accommodated.

Developed in the late 1600s as a low chest with drawers, the commode became extremely popular in France from the mid-1700s on.

The French word *"commode"* means practical, so a commode was made for wherever you needed some drawers. There are corner commodes, bedside commodes, dining room commodes (*commode-dessert*), etc.

In America, the word "commode" came to mean another practical piece of furniture, the potty chair. The French call that convenience a "chaise percée," meaning "chair with a hole in it." Very unglamorous of the French.

Whatnot/Etagere

The whatnot, everybody knows, is where Victorians displayed all the thingamajigs and whatjamacallits they collected. But why didn't they call it an "*etagere*," as the French did.

"*Etage*" is the French word for step, and an *etagere* does have shelves or steps for display. But the word *"etagere"* is usually reserved for larger wall or corner pieces. A whatnot, while it can be a hanging piece or a corner piece, is invariably smaller, may have as few as two shelves, and is often freestanding. Whatever.

In Old Vienna

Wise collectors and decorators have long realized what has become more and more popularly accepted today: One hundred years ago it was Vienna, not London, Paris or New York, that was the cultural and intellectual capital of the world.

Vienna was the capital of the Austro-Hungarian Empire (1867–1918) and its motto was, *"Wissen macht frei,"* "Knowledge liberates." It was the first modern progressive city of the 20th Century, creating public schools, hospitals, and a system of public assistance to the needy.

It was the city of Sigmund Freud, who not only invented psychoanalysis, but revolutionized literature and all the arts in the process.

In music, while Johann Strauss was creating the waltz, and a whole new approach to popular music, composers like Mahler, Schoenberg and Berg, were advancing music in ways we are still coming to terms with today.

But what does this have to do with antiques? The answer lies in another Viennese term, *"Gesamtkunstwerk,"* meaning "total work of art." This was the theory that each of the arts should reflect all of the arts and that all of the arts should be reflected in industry, education, civic planning and even interior design.

So, the best decorative arts produced in turn-of-the-century Austria will truly evoke their time and place, which is our criterion for what makes the very best in antiques.

For instance, pictures and figures of the human face and form are common in the Austrian decorative arts of that day, especially on hand-painted and transferware porcelains and in bronze statuary.

Notice these people. See how unapologetically real and lively they are. Even classical and mythological figures have distinct personalities—introspective, optimistic, intelligent, often caught on the verge of action, speech, laughter, awareness.

Florals are executed as you might see blooms in nature, with all the organic intensity of blossoms drawn forth by the sun and blown by the wind. Border decorations, embossing and gilding, even on the most formal pieces of pottery, porcelain and art glass, literally seem to dance.

Look for porcelains marked Royal Vienna, Royal Austria, Victoria, Carlsbad, M. Z., O&EG (with any of the various blue "beehive" marks, actually a shield taken from the Emperor's coat of arms), or the fantastic art pottery of Amphora, Turn-Teplitz, Bohemian and Royal Dux factories of the same kingdom.

Colorful pieces signed Kaufmann on the front are very collectible. They are not hand painted, however, but are transferware representations of romanticized classical scenes by the 18th Century artist, Angelica Kauffmann.

Bohemian art glass creations, especially from Ludwig Moser and Johann Loetz, are highly prized as are the exotic bronzes of Bergman (sometimes signing backwards, "Nam Greb," especially on naughty pieces), and the Viennese Werkstadt.

The Austrian empire collapsed after World War I, but I think their natural introspection helped the Viennese understand that it was just time for it all to be over. In the end, it was knowledge that freed Vienna.

These Three Kings

When Karl Lagerfeld, the famous fashion designer, was asked (in a *Vogue* magazine profile questionnaire) to list his favorite names, he answered, "Louis XIV, Louis XV and Louis XVI."

These three kingly styles of French furniture have long been favorites among people of wealth and taste and every fifty years or so they become popular favorites as well.

Now is one of those times.

The Louis styles are often referred to simply by the French words for the numerals after each king's name—Quatorze (14), Quinze (15) and Seize (16) and pronounced, respectively, "kat-ORZ," "Kanz" and "Says."

Original pieces in any of these styles are rare and costly. All three, however, have been produced as French revival styles during the mid-19th Century, at the turn of the century and in the mid-20th Century, and all can be found in today's antique shops.

Louis XIV (1643-1715) was the "Sun King" who built Versailles, and all the furniture named after him is in the Baroque style—heavy, masculine, ornately carved and regal (some say pompous). Chairs are throne-like, especially the armchairs. In this Louis' court, only the king's chairs could have arms.

Look for X-shaped stretchers or figure-eight shapes connecting the legs. There may also be some ormolu (gilt metal) decoration, especially sunbursts and the mythical sun god, Apollo.

Quatorze has been the least successful as a revival style. The furniture was made for palaces, so it was just too palatial, too heavy and massive even for grand homes.

Louis XV (1715-1774) is decidedly a more feminine style, perhaps due to the influence of the king's famous mistress, Madame Pompadour. The lines of this furniture are all continuous, sweeping, exaggerated curves. In all, however, it's a much more comfortable style than Louis XIV.

Quinze is a Rococo style, with deep carving, sometimes in openwork, and including floral decorations. Frames can be gilt, or painted in soft tones of white, blue or green.

Of all the Louis styles, this is probably the most beautiful, and it was a huge hit with the Victorians, so it is still available in the shops, especially the gilt pieces. I'd have to agree with those who conclude that Louis XV revival is some of the best furniture the Victorians produced.

French Provincial style was also developed during the Louis XV period. While somewhat heavier than regular Quinze style, the curvaceous lines remain.

Provincial was a big revival style in the 1950s, and although much of the mass-produced pieces came off clunky and unattractive, you can find some really fine 50s Provincial furniture, especially if it was custom-made.

Louis XVI (1774-1792) may have lost his head, but the neo-Classical furniture that bears his name is perhaps the most sane, well-mannered and stylish ever made.

Legs are straight, round, tapered and fluted. Decoration, carved or ormolu, includes Greco-Roman designs like scrolls, caryatids, key-designs, swags and garlands. Everything is rectilinear, symmetrical, sometimes even architectural.

Am I gushing?

Well, this is a truly elegant style, so sensible and graceful that both men and women love it. It's timeless, even in the most modern environment, and it was a strong influence on the best modern designers from the 1930s through the 1950s.

Seize is always popular, but it had particularly strong revivals in the late Victorian and turn-of-the-century periods as well as the mid-20th Century.

By the way, the witty Mr. Lagerfeld speaks six languages, and his men's cologne is quite good. Smart man, and smarter, too, to love all those old Looeys.

The Secret Of Eastlake's Success

"Eastlake" is the name given to the style that dominated the huge middle-class market in furniture and interior decoration during the last thirty years of the 19th Century, at the end of the Victorian Age.

The technical term for the style is "Reformed Gothic," but it became known as "Eastlake" because of the dramatic influence of a little book, "Hints on Household Taste, in Furniture, Upholstery and Other Details," published in London in 1868 (American edition, 1872) by a 32-year-old architect, Charles Locke Eastlake.

What was it about this book that made it so powerfully influential it immortalized its author's name?

At least part of the answer can be found in the author's own words in the preface to his book, where he declares his purpose "to suggest some fixed principles of taste for the popular guidance of those who are not accustomed to hear such principles defined."

Eastlake wants to reach out to a broad range of people. Notice also that he calls his work, "Hints," and says his purpose is "to suggest." This lack of pretension permeates his book, and is what made it then, and makes it now, so easy to understand.

Tastemakers can be tyrants, snobbish, and absolute in their pronouncements about what we should and shouldn't like. While Eastlake is firm in his convictions about what is and isn't good design, he believes that his conclusions are based on a kind of simple common sense anyone can comprehend.

During Eastlake's time, the great debate in architecture and design was between the Gothic (Medieval) and Classical (Greco-Roman) schools. And although Eastlake was a confirmed Gothicist, he refused to be dictatorial in his convictions, and incorporated elements of both schools in his design ideas.

He writes: "I recommend the re-adoption of no specific type of ancient furniture which is unsuited, whether in detail or general design, to the habits of modern life."

While Eastlake designed furniture (as well as wallpaper, metal wares and jewelry), he never actually made furniture. But furniture makers in both England and the U.S. were cashing in on Eastlake's popularity by marketing "Eastlake" furniture.

Real Eastlake furniture is useful and practical, and its beauty is found in the simple elegance of the design. Although some mirrors will be topped with a decorative crown, most decoration is carved into a piece, rather than applied to it.

Eastlake preferred the realness of oak and the warmth of walnut to the slickness of mahogany, and would opt for black stain (ebonized) finishes rather than the high luster of French polish.

The classic Eastlake table is the oval or rectangular occasional table, so named because it can be used anywhere in the home for a variety of functions. The table stands on a center post bracketed with four, carved wing-shaped legs. The top is usually marble and has an apron, usually carved. With so-called "picture-frame tables," the marble top is framed with wood.

Eastlake's upholstered parlor chairs and settees traditionally show a great deal of wood often with openwork carving on top and "trumpet" feet—a large knob at top tapering at the bottom and sometimes finished with metal or porcelain rolling casters.

For period designer furniture, Eastlake pieces are among the most available and affordable on the market-a real bargain. Occasional tables range from $450 to $900, cane seat dining chairs from $150 to $250 each, upholstered armchairs $350 to $600, and armless (or demi-arm) ladies' chairs from $200 to $300. Upholstered and caned pieces will be much less if they have to be re-done.

You can still get a copy of "Hints on Household Taste." The Dover reprint of the 4th (1878) edition has been republished and is available in most bookstores. Get a copy. It's still a great read.

Art Deco—The Past As The Future

During a trip to Florida I made yet another pilgrimage to the Art Deco district in the South Beach section of Miami Beach. This time it was Art Deco Weekend and the famous strip on Ocean Drive was closed to traffic and lined with vendors' tents and food stalls.

There was no question that there was quite a festival going on.

The oceanfront boulevard was packed with people—jammed shoulder to shoulder in sidewalk cafes; dancing in the streets to loud Latin music; having their pictures taken with clowns, drag queens and other local eccentrics; congregating around the spot in front of Versace's mansion where the famous designer was murdered; munching on aerepas and tacos and corn dogs and barbecued chicken.

They were also buying antiques, posters and original artwork, old and new postcards, advertising art and Art Deco reproductions.

And no money was spared on the event's free program—a 40-page glossy magazine with a cover featuring the Weekend's outrageous official poster (a dancing girl in a banana skirt holding the Eiffel Tower in one hand and a beret in the other) and the words, "Paris 1925/Miami Beach 2000—75 Years of Art Deco."

To be sure, there was lots about this festival that had little to do with Art Deco, but the city certainly had something to celebrate: Art Deco has been very, very good to Miami Beach. And beyond the food smells and the din of the crowd, you could almost imagine the elegant Jazz Age couples descending from these stately, brightly colored hotels into their awaiting Hudson limousines.

It all started when a fire burned down a large portion of the South Beach area in the mid-1920s. The city fathers, hoping to compete with Palm Beach for the high-class tourist trade from the Northeast, decided to remake Miami Beach in that modern, futuristic new European style that was all the rage among the arty set.

What they meant, of course, was the style that was exhibited in Paris at the 1925 *Exposition Internationale des Arts Decoratifs et Industriels Modernes* (The International Exposition of Modern Decorative and Industrial Arts).

It wasn't yet known by its shortened name, "Art Deco." At that time it was called by various names—Bauhaus, Jugendstil, Esprit Nouveau, and Jazz Age style. The term "Art Deco" wouldn't come into being until 1966, when there was a retrospective of the style at the Paris Museum of Decorative Arts. And it was just about that time that smart collectors began buying it up.

These days the fad for collecting Art Deco has turned into something of a mania. Collectors know the style will be 100 years old and officially antique in 2025, and the 21st Century will look back on Deco as one of the most distinctive styles of the 20th Century.

Except for Miami Beach, America came late to Art Deco. We sent no representatives to the 1925 Paris Exposition, because President Hoover said that American design was "not avant-garde enough."

American would eventually make important contributions to the Art Deco style, including the requisite Jazz music, the skyscraper (like the Chrysler and Empire State Buildings), as well as all the neat stuff from the Chicago World's Fair of 1933 and the 1939 New York World's Fair.

That comment by Hoover, however, shamed some American designers into starting the Chase Copper and Brass Company (oddly, best known for its chrome wares), and all pieces marked "Chase" sell very well on today's market, even in Europe.

You may hear the terms, "Egyptian Art Deco" or "Chinese Art Deco." This refers to the kinds of styles that influenced the Deco designs. The opening of King Tut's Tomb in 1923, for instance, caused a rash of "Tut-mania" in the design world, affecting everything from architecture to fashion and jewelry.

Oriental design also influenced Deco design because of the increased imports from the Orient during the period. Chinese-made rugs, for instance, incorporated their traditional motifs of vases, birds and flowering branches into strikingly Deco designs. And the Japanese fed American five-and-ten-cent stores with a variety of affordable porcelains like ashtrays, kitchen items, vanity pieces, etc., in colorfully hand-painted, Deco-style lusterware.

If you think you have missed the boat on Art Deco, and that there is nothing left to find, think again. There is still plenty on the market that is available and affordable.

Look for Czechoslovakian glass and porcelain from the era, as well as Czech, German and and Japanese lusterwares from the late '20s through the 1930s. Depression glass often reflected the Deco style in patterns like Manhattan and Moderntone.

Besides Chase metalwares, look for American Art Deco in Phoenix and Consolidated Glass, Verlys (made in France and Ohio), Libby, Morgantown and Cambridge glass, especially the American cut rock crystal stemware (1920s-1940s) and other barwares of the period, like cocktail shakers and their magnificent "Statuesque" line, also called "Nude Stem."

In home furnishings, you can still find affordable, Depression-Era American pieces in varying quality. Look particularly at mirrors, lamps and cocktail tables, and especially bedroom sets. Many of the lady's vanities, some decorated with colored glass mirrors, are very strikingly Deco in design.

For Comfort, It's Wicker, Naturally

"… when he swolne and pamper'd with great fare Sits downe and snorts, cag'd in his basket chair."

—John Donne, *Elegie I, On Jealosie*

The olde English may be a struggle, but the image is easy to visualize. We've witnessed it at many a family barbecue—the stuffed and satisfied guest plopping into a comfortable wicker armchair.

Wicker furniture has always been about comfort, even during the 16th Century when this poem was written and wicker chairs were called "peasant chairs," much more comfortable than those hard, straight-backed thrones the aristocracy had to rule from.

The word "wicker" is from the Swedish *wika*, meaning "to bend" and *vikker*, meaning "willow." It is the correct word for all pieces made from woven natural fiber, including rattan, cane, rush, reed, willow, raffia and a variety of dried grasses.

The ancestor of the wicker we know today is the reed and papyrus furniture created by the Egyptians and Sumerians over four thousand years ago. But our wicker is made chiefly from the branches of the rattan palm (*Calamus Rotang*) found in the East Indies and Malaysia.

These branches are so strong that Oriental fishermen wove them into mooring ropes. Malaysians made walking sticks from them. In fact, our word "rattan" comes from the Malaysian word for a cane, *"rotan."*

Victorian wicker furniture got its start one day in 1844, when a struggling Boston grocer, Cyrus Wakefield, sat in that city's harbor watching the ships being unloaded.

He noticed that a large amount of wicker material, used as dunnage to keep crates from banging against one another during shipping, was being carted away as rubbish.

He began by selling the stuff to basket weavers, who would strip off the outer part of the rattan, called "cane," to use the inner reeds. Then he would sell the discarded cane to chair makers to make cane seats for chairs.

Eventually he started the Wakefield Rattan Company, and became the premier "wicker" furniture maker in the country. His chief rival was Heywood Brothers, an old and well-established furniture company.

By 1897 the two companies felt it would be more profitable to work together than to compete. Heywood-Wakefield wicker has long been sought after by Victorian/Edwardian collectors and decorators.

Old wicker can be hard to find and pricey, especially if it is tightly woven and ornately fancy. But the pieces that have stood the test of time are usually the sturdiest and have a wonderful character about them that just can't be duplicated.

Even if you opt for new wicker, and there are some good quality pieces out there, accenting with old wicker pieces can make your whole ensemble that much more charming, breezy and, above all, more comfortable.

An American Original

"Get your happiness out of your work or you will never know what happiness is."

—Elbert Hubbard

The story of the Roycrofters guild and its founder, Elbert Hubbard (1856-1915), contains a key to understanding a uniquely American philosophy that many believe is responsible for this nation's rise to greatness.

Elbert Hubbard was born in Bloomington, Illinois, and came east to find his fortune. He landed in the unlikely city of Buffalo, New York, as a soap salesman for the Larkin Soap Company.

During his tenure at Larkin, Hubbard met and became friendly with the architect of the company's new headquarters, Frank Lloyd Wright. Wright told him of the successful marketing experience of a man in England named William Morris, who was spearheading something called the Arts and Crafts Movement in that country.

Hubbard decided to visit Morris, and came back with an idea to set up a commune of artists and craftsmen to produce affordable, high-quality, handmade items that could compete favorably with the factory-made products of the new industrial age.

He founded the Roycrofters, named for two 17th Century printers, in a suburb of Buffalo, East Aurora. The guild's first products were hand-printed magazines and books expounding Hubbard's philosophy. Before long, artists and craftsmen from all over the country arrived at his doorstep to become part of this new American Art and Crafts Movement.

It was a remarkable success. Americans everywhere loved the simple functional forms and obvious touches of handicraft that characterized Roycroft pieces. Hubbard's soap salesmen skills in direct mail and catalogue marketing helped to sell the guild's products in the most remote regions of the country. His craftsmen even developed furniture, like bookcases and magazine racks, that could be sent through the mail and assembled in the home.

Roycroft products became quite fashionable. People felt they were not only buying furniture or decorative accessories, but a philosophy. That philosophy, however, drew fire from some jealous new-capitalist factory owners. Guilds like the Roycrofters were accused of being socialist and later communist. This detraction wasn't helped by William Morris who spoke vigorously, when on tour in America, on behalf of this country's fledgling labor movement.

But Hubbard's philosophy was hardly unpatriotic. It was as American as Benjamin Franklin and his "Poor Richard's Almanac."

It has been called "American Pragmatism," an optimistic philosophy often delivered in epigrams, sayings, truisms and mottoes, advice to live by like "A penny saved is a penny earned," and "Rarely use venery (sex) except for health or offspring," and "A stitch in time saves nine." It

seems so simple, shallow and even silly. But it has been a working philosophy in America for over 200 years.

The eminent American poet and essayist, Ralph Waldo Emerson,
incorporated the philosophy into religion as a Unitarian minister.
Other ministers followed, like the Reverend Norman Vincent Peale,
who wrote the best-selling book, "The Power of Positive Thinking,"
and the Revered Shuler, whose sermons from his Crystal Cathedral in
California became a television ratings phenomenon for religious pro-
gramming.

William James, the American philosopher and brother of the novel-
ist, Henry James, introduced the philosophy to Harvard and the aca-
demic world. His essay, "The Moral Equivalent of War," was the
inspiration for John F. Kennedy's establishment of the Peace Corps.

It was Hubbard, however, who introduced Franklin's pragmatic philosophy into the world of business and marketing. There may have
been others, but it was Hubbard who wrote it down and put it into
practice at his Roycrofters guild. No one would do that more vigorously until the 20th Century and Dale Carnegie's huge best-selling
salesman's bible, "How to Win Friends and Influence People."

Since then, this philosophy has been used and abused by a myriad of
twelve-step programs and commercial enterprises from Alcoholics
Anonymous to "The Lazy Man's Way to Riches." It has helped people
kick drug habits, be better managers, sell more real estate, improve
memories, get top grades in school, and spawned a host of other
believe-in-yourself, do-it-yourself, confidence-building programs for
self-betterment.

This pragmatic philosophy grew out of necessity in America. It became the survival kit for democracy, a hard and unforgiving results-oriented way of taking responsibility for your own happiness for the first people on earth to declare that they truly wanted to rule themselves.

Hubbard combined this with Morris's ideas of the supremacy of quality goods handcrafted by good, happy people at one with the world of nature. Things made by people with people in mind could never be duplicated by any industrial machine. "Do your work with your whole heart," Hubbard wrote in his *Note Book*, "and you will succeed—there is so little competition."

Here are some more of Hubbard's epigrammatic words of wisdom:

"Your friend is the man who knows all about you, and still likes you."

"The greatest mistake you can make in life is to be continually fearing you will make one."

"The best preparation for good work tomorrow is to do good work today."

The Roycroft mark usually consists of an intertwined "RC" in a circle topped with a vertical line crossed by two horizontal bars. On furniture, you will often see a triangular metal tag. Look for these marks, not only on high-quality American antiques, but as an inspiration for everything you do.

It's All Done With Mirrors

Mirrors have long been associated with mystery and magic. Alice walked through the looking glass into a very strange world; the wicked Queen in Snow White sought evil wisdom from the mirror on her wall; vampires couldn't see their own image in a mirror; and if you broke a mirror, you'd be in for lots of bad luck—seven years' worth.

The reason mirrors were so shrouded in mystery is because they were so rare for so many centuries. Among us simple folks, mirrors were quite unfamiliar, and the unfamiliar is often a source of superstition.

There is no mystery today about the popularity of elegant and charming old mirrors. They are very popular on the antiques market, and their history is almost as fascinating as the fairy tales.

In the 1500s, the world center of mirror-making was the Italian city of Venice. By this time, the technology already existed for "silvering" glass. Actually the substance used was not silver, but a combination of tin and mercury. What was missing, however, was the technology to make glass in large, thin, even plates that wouldn't distort the image in the mirror.

Mirrors were produced by blowing a large glass bubble, puncturing the bubble at each end to flatten it, and then grinding it smooth. It was a cumbersome, imperfect, and very labor-intensive process.

By the mid-1600s, England was producing mirrors of its own, chiefly by Sir Robert Mansell, Duke of Buckingham, at his factory in Vauxhall. The glass was still imperfect and to this day the term "Vauxhall" is sometimes used to describe any scruffy old mirror, although it's correctly used only in reference to mirrors made by the old bubble method.

By the late 1600s, the French had greatly improved mirror-making by casting the glass in a metal casing and allowing it to cool slowly. Their crowning achievement was the creation of the Hall of Mirrors (Galerie de Glaces) at Versailles for Louis XIV in 1682.

The King of France may have had many mirrors, but in all of the American colonies at this time, there were probably fewer than 100 mirrors, a figure arrived at by a survey of personal diaries, bills of lading, wills and other documents.

Mirrors were called looking glasses until the early 1800s. The earliest mirrors were displayed in the parlor, where visitors could see them and be impressed. The most common placement was the chimney mirror above the fireplace mantel. A large pier mirror was hung on the wall at the pier beam, the main beam of the house between the two front windows.

In 1840, just as the Victorian Era was dawning, the German, J. von Liebig, created a sharper image by adding real silver to the backing. And by the middle of that decade, mass production of good quality mirrors was well underway.

There was no problem getting customers. As soon as those upwardly mobile Victorians realized how easily they could own something that was once only affordable to the very wealthy, the demand for mirrors soared.

Mirrors were status symbols in the 19th Century. One of the first places Victorians chose to put a mirror was in the foyer or entrance hall, so guests and visitors could see it right away. These mirrors were often very large, sometimes a small seat was attached, or a console table with a card tray, and there were often hooks for hats and coats.

Mirrors appeared everywhere in the Victorian home—vanity mirrors, girandole (mirror sconces with lights), cheval mirrors (freestanding, adjustable dressing mirrors), and whole walls decorated in mirrors with interesting frames.

Frames were designed for all the Victorian revival styles—wrought iron gothic styles, renaissance, Elizabethan, fancy, gilt Louis XV baroque, etc.—as well as their own period styles, like Eastlake, Arts and Crafts, and Art Nouveau.

Above all, Victorians loved reproductions of the frames that would have graced the homes of the wealthy a century earlier, particularly highly carved Chippendale frames, and Queen Anne-style mirrors that were "japanned" (artfully painted lacquer).

Also look for Victorian and turn-of-the-century mirrors with frames that include reverse painted glass, prints, molded chalk or carved limestone plaques, carved wood, silver, bronze and fancy molded brass.

Keep the old glass in old mirror frames whenever possible, unless you need the mirror for practical purposes (like in the bathroom), or if the old glass is truly unsightly, or the fanciness of the frame really cries out for expensive beveled glass.

To test if you have an original mirror glass, put the point of a pencil to the glass. The depth of the image is the thickness of the glass. A shallow image indicates a thinner, older glass.

The more you look at the old mirrors in antiques shops, the more you just may see yourself collecting them. And the decorating possibilities are endless, even in the most contemporary settings. You don't have to be a magician. It's all done with mirrors.

Through The Gargoyle's Eye

When I was a senior in high school, I wrote a column in the school newspaper called "Through the Gargoyle's Eye." It was named for those hideous, long-necked beasts that glowered and snarled at us, during our tender pubescent years, from the exterior and inner courtyards of the turn-of-the-century "Flemish Gothic" building where we learned our Latin well—or else.

I didn't name the column. It had been a tradition in the newspaper for decades as a column of humor and satire, a place where some scapegoat senior of fledgling literary talent could innocently sneer, smirk and be snide, making fun of cafeteria food and faculty foibles. It was an opportunity for us collectively to growl back at those gargoyles.

I hadn't thought of gargoyles much since then, so you can imagine my surprise, on a visit to the supermarket, to find shelves lined with cans of Franco-American "Gargoyles," pastas in sauce (which can be had with or without meatballs). That same week I received an interior design catalogue featuring nothing but gargoyles—in garden sculpture, lamp bases, finials, paperweights, etc.

Then comes my *Time* magazine, with a short feature, "Gargoyles in America," followed by my copy of *The New Yorker,* with a cartoon (uncaptioned) of gargoyles wind-surfing on the River Styx as Charon poles his ferry-load of souls into Hades.

Over the years, gargoyles make periodic comebacks. These grotesque, mythical beasts are now sharing public fascination with the choirs of angels that have been so popular these last few years.

It seems to have started with the kids. Disney has an animated series of gargoyle cartoons on TV with, of course, the requisite licensed toys. There are many other toys and books for children featuring gargoyles, including stuffed toys for tots. And now the kids can eat up the nasty creatures right from the can.

The word "gargoyle" comes from the Old French, meaning throat. Their long throats were used in architecture as run-off ducts to syphon rain from the roofs of old buildings. The word is a distant ancestor of our word "gargle."

Although we associate gargoyles with the cathedrals of the Middle Ages, these figural drain pipes were used much earlier. They can be found on the ancient Greek Parthenon, as well as on the fanciful buildings of Pompeii in Italy.

Since the Middle Ages, the word "gargoyle" has become synonymous with the beasts themselves, and is even incorrectly used for the other nonfunctioning figures that decorate old buildings.

Those figures are technically called "chimeras," after a female character in Greek mythology who is usually depicted as a combination of animals, primarily the lion and the goat, a sort of variation on the Egyptian Sphinx.

While we are on the subject, we might as well mention the griffin (or griffon), who looks like a dog with wings, but is actually supposed to be a combination of eagle, lion and dragon.

These beasts were all an intricate part of what we call the "gothic" architecture and design of the Middle Ages. The Goths were the pagan tribes of central Europe. When they were converted to Christianity, the cathedrals were built not only to celebrate but to instruct. Arches and windows pointed upward to pull the mind away from this world toward heaven; the stained glass windows were rich with religious characters and stories.

The gargoyles played a part, too. The grotesque menagerie on the outside was meant to serve as a contrast to the peace and serenity to be found on the inside, the world of man versus the spiritual world. Because they were used by the Church, they became associated with the stature and authority of that institution, and soon these design elements began showing up in personal and governmental architecture.

The elements of gothic design are important to antiquers today because they were a major part of design during the Gothic Revival of the Victorian and Edwardian eras. The revival started in about the 1850s, and continued up to the First World War. Since this period was roughly 100 to 150 years ago, much of its design is what makes up the antiques market today.

The newly rich Victorians associated gothic design with the old rich aristocracy, who could trace their ancestors way back to the Middle Ages. They incorporated the designs into their decor to make their homes more like their castles.

Like the Victorians, the turn-of-the-century Edwardians also used angels and gargoyles in design (they seemed to be partial to the griffon), and added a host of other mythological nymphs, fairies and pixies. It may have been their way of facing the unknown at the beginning of the brave new world of the 20th Century.

For much of this century, people have avoided gothic design as too busy, distracting and ornate. Now as we face the 21st Century, angels and gargoyles have returned. Whatever the social implications, the designs make interiors—furniture and accessories—rich, historic and interesting.

When visiting the shops, look for the lions holding rings in their teeth, ram's head handles, cherubs embossed on the borders of plates, and the whole array of beasts and beings that decorate the furniture and decorative objects of the past. They are usually hand-carved or hand-crafted, and are always, at least, the product of imaginative and pains-taking design.

Take it from someone who grew up with gargoyles, and has even looked through the gargoyle's eye. They don't bite. They're really quite harmless. And if they make you growl back at the world from time to time, so much the better.

PART II
Stories About Asian Antiques

The Treasures Of The Sindia * Blue And White—From Ballast To First Class * Nanking Gets Clobbered * The Virtues Of Jade * The Mystery Of Celadon * That's Imari * The Gentlemen From Japan * Netsukes And Other Ivories * Monkeying Around

The Treasures Of The Sindia

No matter where I go to appraise things in South Jersey, someone always has something they claim came from the wreck of the Sindia.

On December 15, 1901, the Sindia, a 379-foot, 4-masted, steel-hulled barque, one of the last commercial sailing vessels before steam, plowed into the sand 150 yards from the beach between 16th and 17th Streets in Ocean City.

The ship was en route to New York City from Kobe, Japan. Besides its cargo of chemicals (manganese, camphor, linseed oil, etc.), the Sindia was laden with 5 cases of decorative Oriental screens and (get this) 3,315 cases of "curios," as the manifest called them, including fine Oriental porcelain and pottery, destined to stock store shelves for the last minute rush of Christmas shoppers.

Christmas came early that year for many of the merchants and ordinary folks of Ocean City.

When the Sindia ran aground, its hull cracked, filling with sand and water. At low tide, anyone could walk out to inspect the wreck and loot its cargo.

The objects that were taken from the wreck of the Sindia were among the most popular Oriental decorative and tablewares of the day.

These included Imari and Kutani porcelains, Satsuma pottery and Satsuma-style porcelains, moriage (relief-decorated) and gold-luster tea sets, chocolate sets, various other table services, like nut sets and celery sets, vanity pieces, colorful Geisha ware, and blue and white Phoenix ware.

Besides Oriental style wares, there were also many pieces richly decorated with Western style designs and marked, "Nippon," a word meaning "sunrise," the Japanese name for Japan.

Those who held on to at least some of their booty are often shocked to discover the high prices their things are fetching in today's antique shops.

The same people are often disappointed, however, to learn that their things are no more valuable because they were taken from the Sindia.

Quality and artistry are key elements in pricing the Oriental wares of this period, and the more elaborate the decoration, the more valuable the piece.

Large Imari vases now can be $1,500 to $ 2,500 and chargers from $800 to $2,000 or more. Satsuma urns average from $500 to well over $1,000. Teasets can be $250 to $350. If the bottoms of the cups have pictures, called "lithophanes," one cup and saucer set alone can be $25 to $30.

To discover more about the Sindia, visit the Ocean City Historical Museum in Ocean City, New Jersey. Here's are just some of the fascinating facts you will learn there:

The Sindia was owned by John D. Rockefeller's Anglo-American Oil Company and was of British registry. Although it was carrying over $1.2 million in cargo, it was only insured for $500,000.

The ship was named for Magadee Sindia, Emperor of Hindustan from 1741 to 1749.

All 33 seamen were rescued from the wreck. The Scottish captain, Allan MacKenzie, had his license suspended for six months and never commanded a commercial vessel again.

The Sindia now lies underneath an estimated 10 to 20 feet of sand. Several attempts have been made to excavate it, because it was believed to have been carrying a secret cargo of treasure looted from a Buddhist temple in China.

That treasure, if it ever existed, has never been unearthed, but the treasures that have been saved from the wreck of the Sindia will be forever cherished by the old families of South Jersey.

Blue And White—Ballast To First Class

"My sole ambition," Oscar Wilde once said, "is to live up to my blue and white china."

Wilde never let his poetic license expire, but it's no exaggeration to say that the English speaking world has long had a love affair with Oriental blue and white wares.

Don't believe me? Then here is some more lyric praise from the poet, Andrew Lang (1844-1912), who actually wrote a "Ballad of Blue China":

"There's a joy without canker or cork.

There's pleasure eternally new.

'Tis to gloat on the glaze and the mark

Of china that's ancient and blue."

Lang's lines might be a bit lame (the "canker" here is apparently a crab, the edible crustacean), but otherwise they might also have been written today. Chinese blue and white Canton and Nanking porcelain wares have become very popular again. Collectors and decorators are realizing that for the age, quality and beauty of these wares, they are among the best buys on the antiques market.

The irony is that Canton and Nanking were often stored in cargo hulls as ballast to weigh down and steady the ships that were transporting them to the West. Now they are traveling first class, as elegant decorative accessories in tasteful homes everywhere.

Actually, from their first appearance in the West in the late 1600s, both Nanking and Canton porcelain were extremely popular, especially in the U.S. and England. The enormous volume exported to fill that demand is why these wares were useful as ballast.

Nanking, named for its city of export, was the first to arrive, and Canton came shortly afterwards. Both designs are similar, featuring a scene with some or all of the following elements: trees, clouds, mountains, pagodas, houses, a teahouse, boats and bridges.

The difference between the two patterns lies with the quality of the porcelain, the execution of the design and, most distinctively, in the border patterns.

Canton is considered the cruder of the two. The porcelain is usually heavier. The glaze is less consistent, with blues running from light grayish to cobalt. And the painting is often so primitive it is almost childlike.

If you examine the Canton pattern closely, you can sometimes see a human figure through the window of one of the houses.

The distinctive Canton border is called "Rain and Clouds," an outer border of diagonal lines and an inner border of wavy lines.

The Nanking border is called "Post and Spear," or sometimes, "Spear and Dart." It consists of an outer border over the blue in a lattice-like geometric diamond pattern and an inner border of alternating lines and arrows.

If there is a human figure in the Nanking scene, you will see her on the bridge with an umbrella.

Nanking is a finer porcelain, and the glaze and painting are executed with more attention to detail. Unlike Canton, Nanking was sometimes trimmed with gold.

Despite the fineness of Nanking, Canton wares became the more popular. Westerners seemed to find the crude, primitive decoration more real and charming. Canton was particularly popular in America. George Washington displayed a collection of Canton at Mount Vernon.

In America the demand for Chinese blue and white, especially Canton, continued and was never stronger than between 1880 and World War I. Pieces from this era are still very available on today's antiques market, and so prices are still fairly reasonable.

Canton, Nanking and other Oriental wares are not only important in their own right, but understanding them is the key to understanding many old European decorative arts.

Nanking, for instance, was the inspiration for the development of the popular English Blue Willow pattern. In fact, the first English pattern named "Willow" was called "Willow Nanking," created by Minton in 1790.

Nanking Gets Clobbered

No, that's not a sports headline, just another interesting fact about blue and white Nanking porcelain.

Between 1800 and 1850 some pieces of Nanking ware were additionally decorated with multi-colored flowers and leaves. This is called "Clobbered Nanking," and it is very rare and highly prized.

Why the term "clobbered" is used here has always been a mystery to me. You never know where research into antiques will take you, even into the fascinating world of word origins.

"Clobber" is a word of unknown origin, but most likely Dutch. It means a clump of sticky mud. Our word "to clobber" probably first meant to be spattered with clobbers. The patchy color decoration on Clobbered Nanking is spattered here and there in no particular order.

The Virtues Of Jade

Not since the 1920s have Oriental furnishings and decorative arts been as popular as they are today, and nothing says the Orient like jade.

The Chinese, especially, have revered jade. Confucius compared the virtues of jade to human virtues—purity, intelligence, and justice—and concluded, "Its color represents loyalty, its interior flaws, always showing themselves through the transparency, call to mind sincerity, its iridescent brightness represents heaven."

For the Chinese, such philosophical lyricism about jade is no overstatement. For them, jade is nothing less than health, wealth, strength, beauty and truth. Jade is the ancient material of their first currency, weapons and tools, predating the Bronze Age, before 3000 B.C.

This partially explains the magnificent objects the Chinese created in jade and the patience and painstaking craftsmanship needed to create them.

Jade is too hard to be carved, so it must be sawn, ground and continuously polished into shape.

Jade is actually two distinctly different stones: nephrite (amphibole jade), a silicate of calcium and magnesium, and jadeite (pyroxene jade), a silicate of sodium and aluminum.

They are generally indistinguishable to sight or touch, which is why it has taken thousands of years to recognize the difference.

We get the word "jade" from the Spanish, *piedras de yjado*, meaning "stones for the side," indicating the far-ranging belief that jade had curative powers for nephritic (kidney-related) disorders; thus the word "nephrite."

Ironically, it's the elements in the jadeite, not the nephrite, which are historically credited with kidney health.

It was a typographical error in French that turned *l' ejade* into *le jade*, turning a feminine noun into a masculine one and giving us the word we use today.

The popular bright green jade, mostly seen in beads and other jewelry, is always jadeite. It only occurs in patches of chromium traces in the stone, and is usually surrounded by a cloudy, off-colored white, sometimes called by the unfortunate English nickname, "mutton fat jade," often used in items like hair ties and lamp finials.

Both jade stones come in a variety of colors, including pale mauve, light blue, dark green (spinach jade), yellow, grey and a wide range of greens and browns.

What is sometimes called "black jade" is actually the very dark green of a third and seldom seen variety of jade called chloromelanite.

The most common jade substitutes are chrysoprase, a green-colored variety of chalcedony, and soapstone. Both are lighter and softer than jade. Green glass will not have the natural inclusions found in jade and will also be lighter in weight.

The Chinese were so enamored of jade they created celadon, among the earliest porcelain glazes, a color that celebrates the wide range of greens seen in jade. In all its variety of tints, celadon is among today's most popular decorating colors.

The Mystery Of Celadon

✦

And Other Inscrutable Chinese Colors

Celadon is a shade of green that comes in such a variety of hues that it is not so much a shade as a color unto itself. Essentially, it is a green with a tint of gray, but it can be very pale or as dark as pea soup in tones from lime to olive.

I'm sure all that sounds very unappetizing, but celadon is truly a wonderful color, magical and exotic. I confess, I am a sucker for it.

Celadon is so simple and yet so very rich. It fascinates those of us who love it, because it looks like a real and natural color yet there is something unearthly about it.

The color celadon is named for a type of green-glazed Oriental ware of the same name. The Chinese call it *qingei* (greenish porcelain). So, why do we call it celadon?

The name comes from the character, Celadon, in an 18th Century pastoral romance, "L'Astree" ("The Star Maiden"), by the French play-wright, Honore d'Urfe. Throughout the play, each time the Celadon character appears, he is wearing a different costume, each in a different shade of green.

But who would name a Chinese ceramic after a character in a French play?

A French Jesuit priest named Pere Jacquemart is responsible. He and others of his order were sent to China by the pope to scrutinize the inscrutable East, and maybe make a few converts along the way. Jacquemart's task was to make some sense out of all the wares the Chinese were exporting to the West.

Jacquemart decided to classify the ceramics by their dominant color. For the polychromes (multicolored ware) he created families of color. "Famille rose," or pink family, is the most famous. It includes the popular Rose Medallion pattern, featuring not roses but pink peonies. But there are also famille jaune (yellow), famille verte (green) and famille noire (black).

The monochromes (single-color wares) posed another problem. The Chinese had created glazes in colors never seen before in the West. To call them simply green, red, blue, purple, black, etc. would be misleading. These colors were unique, and required special, descriptive names.

There is an array of different reds, which Jacquemart named for the blood of various animals—pigeon, cow and chicken. (It sounds better in French.) There is also a variety of blues, most commonly the peacock blue that fades from navy to powder.

The purple he called aubergine, French for eggplant, but it's not the dark color of the commonly seen vegetable, more of a light mauve.

The black, originally called "Tete de Negre" (head of the Negro) is now called Mirror Black. Probably the most expensive of the monochromes, it is a remarkably black black, produced from layers of a brown color, which can be sometimes visible at the rims and other extremities.

There is a legend that an ancient Chinese emperor created celadon because he believed he was being poisoned and was convinced that celadon dishes would reveal the presence of poison in his food and drink.

The most likely reason for the creation of the celadon glaze was to imitate a certain shade of jade, a gemstone that comes in a wide range of colors, deepening from white to green to brown and black. The greens define the stone, however, and it's those greens that celadon celebrates.

It's not a hard and fast rule, but the Chinese often painted celadon pieces by applying enamels thickly to create a decoration in relief. Japanese celadon, on the other hand, is mostly painted flatly on the porcelain.

Authentic Chinese celadon may be unmarked before 1850, or marked with a blue stamp of Chinese characters between 1850 and the 1890s. Early 20th Century pieces are marked "China." After the 1920s, you should find "Made in China."

The wonderful thing about celadon is that it goes with every other color. No matter how many times you paint your rooms different colors or change your rugs or upholstery, your celadon pieces will stand there, stately and serene, fitting in yet standing out, like a fine work of art. There is nothing quite like it.

That's Imari

Japanese Imari is the only ceramic ware the Chinese ever copied from anyone. During the 18th and 19th Centuries, it was all the rage among the best families throughout Europe and America. And today it is the most collected of all Oriental porcelains, including the well respected Chinese Rose Medallion.

The reason for Imari's allure is the richness of the colors and designs. The traditional or "Old Japan" colors of Imari are blue, red and gold. The blue is called "gosu" in Japanese. It is produced with a cobalt or indigo pigment and can range from a purplish blue-black to sapphire to gray-blue.

Imari blue is an underglaze color, that is, it is painted directly on the pre-fired bisque (unglazed porcelain) before a piece is glazed and fired again. All other colors are painted over the glaze.

The distinctive red color on Imari is a particularly rich Oriental red, resembling a deep orange. Some Imari pieces will also feature bits of other colors, usually green, black, aubergine, and yellow. The addition of gold decoration gives a sparkle to the whole palette.

The most traditional Imari design consists of a central medallion, sometimes featuring a flower basket, surrounded by panels of decoration called reserves. But it is the colors that define Imari; the designs can be as varied as the different artists who created them.

Some Imari designs will include fish, birds, fans, dragons and flowers, usually the chrysanthemum. Some will combine realistic motifs with rather artful abstract variations that may include off-center medallions, swirled reserves, diamonds and coins.

For Westerners, the most popular Imari has been the type called "brocade" (in Japanese, "nishikide"), where the decoration is so dense that hardly any of the background white is visible at all.

The name Imari comes from the port city where it was believed that most of this style ware was exported. Historians now believe that Nagasaki was the most likely port of export.

In any event, Imari was not produced in either of those cities but in Arita, a chief city of Japanese porcelain manufacture.

Arita is also the source for other Japanese porcelains, like the fine Nabeshima and Kakiemon wares, sparsely and artistically decorated, which were an inspiration for many Western potters (particularly French Haviland) during the Aesthetic Movement's Japanese craze in the 1880s.

Arita Ware, sometimes called "blue and white Imari," is also highly prized by collectors.

Chinese Imari is mostly indistinguishable from the Japanese Imari, except that the Chinese wares won't have any spur marks on the bottom. Spur marks are tiny indentations in the porcelain left by the supports that held a piece in the kiln when fired.

The most famous of the Imari imitations in the West is the "Old Imari" pattern by England's Royal Crown Derby. Initially created in the late 1700s for King George III, "Old Imari" is among the most expensive dinnerware patterns ever made. It is still being made in limited quantities today.

Several English and other European manufacturers produced their own style of Imari wares, including Meissen, Villeroy, Samson and others. These are recognized by their own peculiar marks.

If you are looking to collect old Japanese Imari, start by consulting reputable dealers who are willing to assert as to age. Most Imari on the market these days is from the mid to late 19th Century.

Value will be determined by the artistry of the decoration, especially if the underside of dishes is also decorated, if there is heavy gold, and if the dishes are scalloped.

Most Japanese Imari pieces are marked only with generic marks like "Good Luck" or "Long Life" in Japanese characters. Especially collectible these days are the artist-signed wares (long, up-and-down blue marks) of the Arita family, Fukagawa, from mid-19th to early 20th Century.

So, if you find yourself swooning over some richly decorated piece of porcelain the next time you visit an antique shop, that's not love, that's Imari.

The Gentleman From Japan

◆

The Remarkable Story of Noritake China

"If you want to know who we are,

We are gentlemen from Japan,

On many a vase and jar,

On many a screen and fan."

With these familiar lines from their operetta, "The Mikado," Gilbert and Sullivan were satirizing what had become quite the craze throughout Europe and America at the time—all things Japanese.

It was a trend that began during what we now call the Aesthetic Movement of the 1880s, and continued until the end of World War I. Its influence could be found everywhere from fine art to the Montgomery Ward catalogue, even in grand opera (Puccini's "Madama Butterfly"). It affected fashion, illustration and, most especially, interior design and decoration.

In November of 1852, President Millard Fillmore sent a small fleet of four naval vessels to Japan. Commodore Matthew Perry, the fleet's commander, was to deliver to the Emperor of Japan, among other small gifts, a rosewood box containing a letter on fine vellum paper sealed in gold.

The president's letter read, in pertinent part, "Your Majesty's subjects are skilled in many arts. I am desirous that our two countries should trade with each other for the benefit of both Japan and the United States."

At that time Japan had been an isolated nation for nearly 300 years. Except for a few select Dutch and Chinese merchants, no one and nothing was allowed in or out of their county. Uninvited foreigners were sentenced to death, and the same fate awaited any Japanese who left the country and attempted to return. It was even forbidden to build or equip a seaworthy vessel capable of sailing beyond Japan's coastal waters.

This was only about 150 years ago. The isolated Japanese economy remained fundamentally agricultural; its society was based on a system of tightly knit clans and strict craftsmen's guilds.

After Perry's visit things moved rapidly for Japanese-American relations. On March 31, 1854, Perry signed the Treaty of Kanagawa, opening Japanese ports to American trade. President Franklin Pierce influenced the U. S. Senate to ratify the treaty the following year.

The Noritake story begins in 1860 with a 22-year-old Japanese baron, Ichizaemon Morimura VI. Morimura was given the responsibility of establishing personal relationships with representatives of foreign governments and their merchants.

In this position, he began to realize how totally outclassed his long-isolated nation was by superior Western industry and commercial savvy. He knew Japan's future would be dim if it couldn't compete in the international marketplace.

Morimura moved immediately. He sent his younger brother, Yukata, abroad to study Western designs and market practices, and established "Morimura Gumi," a pioneer Japanese trading company, in March of 1876. In September of that year, Yukata opened a retail store on Front Street in New York City.

The company traded all sorts of items, but was particularly successful with porcelains. In 1878, Yukata formed the "Morimura Brothers" company with the express intent to produce superior porcelain in Japan for export to the United States.

In 1901, Morimura Brothers established the Noritake company in the Japanese city of Nagoya. The company was named for the old feudal family that had ruled that region in ancient times. Their company logo was an "M" in a wreath; items made between 1891 and 1921 were additionally marked with the word, "Nippon," the Japanese word for Japan.

The Noritake line was an enormous success. Yukata's study of Western-style decorative art really paid off. The company produced fine porcelain dinnerware with French, English and German designs at a fraction of the cost for china from any of those countries.

Throughout Noritake's history, it's commitment to quality was evident, but never so much as during the years immediately following World War II. With the Japanese ceramic industry devastated by the war, the company decided that it couldn't live up to its name. From

1945 until 1948, they marked their wares "Rose China," until they were once again worthy to be called Noritake.

To learn more about this remarkable company, read Joan Van Patten's "The Collectors' Encyclopedia of Noritake China" (Collector Books).

The Morimura brothers were smart, ambitious, imaginative and competetive, but they were also gentlemen. Ichizaemon, an intensely spiritual man, once wrote a six-point "Creed for Our Company." The very first of these points bears noting:

"This company was established in order to recognize the brotherhood of human beings, to keep the peace of the world, to bring happiness to everyone and to practice justice and humanity by means of the foreign trade business."

Not a bad way to get ahead in the world.

Netsukes And Other Ivories

The word "netsuke" is most commonly pronounced "net-skee" in English and "net-skeh" in Japanese. It is a miniature figurine, usually carved in ivory, but also made of various materials like carved wood, coral, silver and other metals.

A netsuke is pierced with two holes, because it functions as a toggle. The Japanese robe, called a kimono, has no pockets, so personal items must be carried in a box-like purse called an inro or sagemono. The inro is attached by a cord strung though the netsuke and looped under the kimono's sash (obi).

This mode of dress prevailed in Japan for over three centuries from the early 1600s until the end of the Mejii period in 1912, when Western fashion started to become more influential.

Beyond their function, however, netsukes are masterful works of art. They are miniature sculptures executed in remarkable detail, and often artist-signed. Their compact size posed a unique challenge to the artist. And because netsukes dangle, they had to be pleasing to the eye from all angles.

Netsukes were created in a variety of shapes during their three centuries of use, but from the end of the 1700s to the early 1900s the most common were the katabori type—realistic representations of humans, animals, plants, and mythological figures—carved in the round. It is this type of netsuke that has attracted collectors for decades.

Many netsukes are based on mythology or folklore, and it's fun to try to find out what the story is. For instance, I recently found a netsuke featuring a man, woman and child. I was puzzled by the position of the child, until I learned that the sculpture was a momotarro group, depicting the story of a couple who couldn't have children but discovered a child inside a nut or peach pit.

The most expensive netsukes will have been sculpted by any one of about 200-300 artists, whose works are well known to specialists in the field and regularly come up for sale at major auctions. There are many beautifully detailed netsukes, however, by lesser known artists, and they are much more affordable. The difference in price is from the thousands to the hundreds of dollars.

Ivory netsukes were carved from elephant, marine or walrus tusks, and while much of it was fossil ivory, chosen for its aged patina, this fact still appalls some folks. The sale and import of new ivory is banned by international agreement these days, however, and what collectors of netsukes celebrate is the craftsmanship and artistry of another time.

Aside from netsukes, this artistry is also exhibited in an array of old Oriental ivory artifacts, such as Japanese "okimono" (complex artistic sculptures, often with religious themes), puzzle balls (How did they carve that ball within a ball within a ball?), cribbage boards, mah jong tiles and chessmen, lamp finials, boxes and other decorative and functional items.

Netsukes and other ivories are so highly sought after that they have been widely reproduced. The new netsukes are a no-brainer—they are angular cut with sharp edges and little remarkable detail.

Ivory has been faked since the late 19th Century with a variety of plastics and resins that can really fool the eye. True ivory is an extremely hard organic material that will have an irregular graining visible under a jeweler's loop. It is also a dense material, and objects will be slightly heavier that you might expect for their size.

Real ivory will also stay cool to the grasp. A small area, burned with a hot pin will exude something of the odor of burning hair. The plastics will smell like plastic.

Since the ban on new ivory, old ivory has become more desirable than ever, and the trend for Oriental decorative arts will be with us for a while. If you don't feel confident enough in the field, make at least your initial purchases from reputable dealers.

Monkeying Around

One of Aesop's fables is based on the ancient belief that dolphins would always come to the rescue of a man in peril at sea.

The story tells of a ship, on which a monkey was aboard, that sinks in a storm. Floating on a piece of flotsam, the monkey spies a passing dolphin and tries to convince it that he's a man, and thus worthy of rescue. The dolphin agrees to carry the monkey on its back, but after asking a few pointed questions, realizes it was fooled and tosses the monkey back into the sea.

Monkeys seem to be human, but they're not. This ambiguity has fascinated people around the world since ancient times, and you can see it reflected in centuries of art and artifacts.

Some cultures view monkeys with disdain, as sort of humans who didn't make it all the way. There is an African myth, for instance, that holds that monkeys, and their simian relatives—apes, baboons, chimpanzees, etc.—descended from lazy tribes that found village life too tedious and decided to return to a more easy going life in the jungle.

The Greeks thought monkeys were the Cercopes, a people punished for playing a joke on Hercules. The Jewish Talmud also speaks of monkeys as punished humans, specifically, as some of the builders of the Tower of Babel.

Other cultures have looked more kindly on monkeys. The Egyptians, for instance, revered the baboon, whom they considered a sibling of man. The falcon, the jackal, the baboon and man were the four children of the god, Horus. Of the four, it is the baboon, not man, who is sacred to Thoth, the god of wisdom.

Buddhist legend holds that the monkey was born on a mountain top from a stone egg miraculously impregnated by Heaven. The Buddha, himself, is said to have been reincarnated as a monkey several times. And it was a monkey who assisted the great monk, Hsuan-tsang, to document the Buddha's teachings for dissemination around the world.

The Chinese particularly admired the aristocratic gibbon, whose reclusive aloofness they associated with the Buddhist ideal of studied disinterest in human affairs.

The Japanese liked the more lively and gregarious macaque, and were the first to dress monkeys in human garb and make them perform, originally for religious rather than entertainment purposes. The ancient belief was that dancing monkeys could cure sick animals.

The Japanese are also responsible for the most well-known of monkey representations—the "see no evil, hear no evil, speak no evil" trio. They even gave them names—Mizaru, Kikarazu and Irawazu. And, like the Chinese, the Japanese believed that the poses of these three monkeys illustrated complete innocence of all human nonsense.

Monkeys have been painted by the great masters with aristocrats, saints and even with the Madonna. They have been sculpted by Michelangelo, cast in bronze, brass and in the finest Meissen porcelain, and included in the decor of some of the most magnificent old residences in continental Europe.

Renewed interest in monkeys and monkey motifs in today's antiques market is the result of a couple of factors. The first is the revival of turn-of-the-century Edwardian decoration with its fondness for exotic animals, especially jungle creatures. The second reason is the rise in popularity of Chinese and Japanese decorative arts in general.

In England and America, monkeys never really conveyed the deep significance and symbolism they had in the rest of the world. We just think they're curious and cute, like children or pets. They make us smile, and that's reason enough for including them in our decor.

Whatever the current reason, however, dealers and collectors have always known that if they found anything monkey-related, they had something very special.

PART III
Stories About Ceramics

Porcelain With A Bit Of English

We call all our dinnerware dishes, "china." Technically, however, the term is reserved for porcelain, because China is where porcelain originated about two thousand years ago. In Japan, they started making porcelain wares about one thousand years ago.

True porcelain is a remarkable gem of a substance, quite an achievement. It's very hard—the French call it, "pate dure," hard paste—and it is much tougher than it seems, especially when it is thick and heavy. But it can be made as delicately thin as an eggshell.

Marco Polo was among the first Europeans to see porcelain and he gave it its name, "porcelana," the Italian name for a cowry shell. (Actually, the seashell is named for the iridescent spines on the back of a wild pig.) Polo called porcelain by that name because of the slick, silky, vitreous surface that it takes on when glazed. Unglazed porcelain is called bisque or biscuit, and it has a roughness that turns velvety with age.

When bisque porcelain is polished, it takes on the quality of fine white marble or alabaster. This is called "parian," and it was common with busts and other statuary. Parian was a Victorian favorite.

Why all this fuss about porcelain? It's because you may have been taking it for granted. Porcelain may be common, but it is far from commonplace. Start noticing it again, especially the European kind.

Europeans only discovered the formula for porcelain about 300 years ago. That formula—a mixture of koalin (china clay) and petuntse (china stone, also called feldspar), fired at 1,300 degrees Fahrenheit—was arrived at by Johann Boettger, a 19-year-old alchemist in the employ of Augustus I, King of Poland and Elector of Saxony, in the city of Dresden in January of 1708. Two years later, the first European porcelain factory began production in the town of Meissen, a suburb of Dresden.

Dresden and Meissen are two names that readily come to mind when thinking of European porcelain. You may also think of other fine German porcelains, like R.S. Prussia, Volkstedt or any of the Bavarian and Austrian companies. You might also consider French Sevres, Old Paris or Limoges.

You are not likely to think about England, however. The English are better known for their Staffordshire pottery wares—the famous dogs, the figurines, Wedgwood's cameo jasperware, "bone china" (from the white ash of burnt ox bones), flow blue, pink luster, etc.—all wonderful things, but not porcelain.

The English came late to porcelain, about the 1740s, and even then it was a soft paste (pate tendre), a thin white earthenware, not as hard as true porcelain. Because they had to import the materials for true porcelain, the English didn't really get into full production until later in the 1790s.

The earliest companies are Bow (pronounced "bo"), Caughley (pronounced "CAR-flee"), Chelsea, Lowestof, Derby (pronounced "DAR-bee") and Worcester (pronounced "WUH-ster"). Other companies that began making English porcelain by the early 1800s include Spode, Machin, Hicks and Meigh, Coalport, Minton, New Hall and several companies in the Liverpool area.

The world of English porcelains is a rarefied one. Except for the Caughley factory that attempted to produce wares for the mass market, most English porcelain was produced for the very wealthy. As a result, they are among the most exquisite porcelains ever made anywhere.

Early Chelsea and Bow figurines, for instance, are among the most rare and sought-after on the antiques market. Derby's Japanese-inspired Imari patterns (there are at least three), are entirely hand-painted. If you are not impressed, go look at some. They are simply awesome. Worcester has a remarkable matte-white glaze that looks very much like antique ivory.

As you might expect, English porcelains are not inexpensive. And the older they are, the more expensive they'll be. But among the porcelains on the market, because they are not so well-known, they can be a bargain.

Casual collectors are put off by the fact that so few early English porcelains are marked. Many late 18th and early 19th Century pieces will only bear a handwritten set of pattern numbers, sometimes written as a fraction. By the mid to late 19th Century most of the fine English porcelain companies marked their wares, and some included some sort of cipher to indicate the date a piece was produced.

To become a member of the rare and exclusive club of English porcelain collectors, it's important to be able to read these marks and ciphers. I suggest starting with two books "Bergesen's British Ceramics" by Victoria Bergesen (Barrie & Jenkins) and "British Ceramic Marks" by J. P. Cushion (Faber & Faber).

The Limousine Of Porcelains

Limousine, the word for a classy, luxurious automobile, comes from a district in France called the Limousin, where the traditional mode of transportation was a horse-drawn, covered carriage with upholstered seats.

The capital city of the Limousin is a name familiar to most of you. It is Limoges, a city that for over 100 years produced the limousine of porcelains, classy and luxurious tableware for the American market.

Limoges had always been a porcelain manufacturing center. It had the requisite deposits of china clay (kaolin), and forests full of trees to fuel the kilns up to those extremely high temperatures that the manufacture of porcelain requires.

But before the French Revolution, porcelain manufacturing in that country was a monopoly controlled by the king in the city of Sevres, or by crown-licensed factories in Paris.

Limoges began to flourish after the Revolution in the late 1700s, and was given a boost in the early 1800s by the patronage of Emperor Napoleon and his first wife, Josephine.

The big break for Limoges, however, would come courtesy of an American, David Haviland. Here's the story:

David and his brother, Daniel, ran a china shop in Manhattan, selling mostly Staffordshire pottery along with some expensive porcelains from England (Worcester, Derby, etc), and Germany (Meissen and Dresden).

One day in the late 1830s, a lady came into their shop with a broken cup that she wanted to replace. She had purchased it in Limoges, she said, and that gave David Haviland an idea.

He had always believed that if porcelain dishes were more affordable, most Americans would prefer them, and Limoges could be the answer. So he took his family to France and in 1842 opened a decorating studio, where he and his artists painted porcelain ordered from the Limoges factories. The dishes were then sent to his brother Daniel for sale in Manhattan.

The plan was a big success, so, in 1867, David opened his own porcelain manufacturing company.

In the 1870s, David's nephew (his brother Daniel's son), Charles Field Haviland, opened his own factory in Limoges. And in the 1890s, David's grandson, Theodore Haviland, opened his own porcelain manufacturing plant.

There are literally hundreds of patterns of Haviland dinnerware, and many of the patterns are very similar. Nancy Schleiger catalogued most of the patterns in six volumes. So if you need to replace pieces and call Replacements Limited, you will be given a "Schleiger" number for your pattern.

However, many folks like to mix and match different Haviland patterns, because they go so well together on the same dinner table or in a cabinet.

The Havilands had opened up the American market for Limoges porcelains, and the family was obviously a huge presence in that city, but they were by no means the only act in town.

Other Limoges companies also produce magnificent hand-painted porcelains for the American market. Some of my favorites include: Charles Ahrenfeldt (CA), Bawo & Dotter (Elite), Bernardaud (B&Co.), Gerard, Dufraisseix and Abbot (GDA, or GDM with Morel), Klingenberg (AK), Jean Pouyat (JP), Lanternier, M. Redon (MR), Tressemann & Vogt (T&V), and several others.

There may be as many as four marks on a piece of Limoges. These would be the maker's mark, the decorator's mark, the importer's mark, and a retailer's mark. Some patterns were made exclusively for a particular retailer. A piece with a "W" in a wreath mark on the bottom, for instance, was made exclusively for Wanamaker's.

Limoges dinnerware is one of the great bargains on the antiques market, especially when you consider that every piece on your table was meticulously painted by hand.

Expect to pay more for a Limoges set if the borders are irregularly shaped, the pieces have all-over painting rather than painting just on the border, if there is a fair amount of gold trim, and if the handles and finials of the serving pieces are fancy shapes, like bows or branches.

Also, expect to pay a premium for special sets, like fish and game sets, punch sets and beverage sets, oyster plates and rare decorative wares, like candlesticks, plaques, vases, cachepots and jardinieres.

Limoges china flooded the American market from 1850 to 1950 and particularly from 1900 to 1925, when it was *the* china cabinet china, the "good dishes," for so many American families.

Belleek: The Luck Of The Irish

There is a legend about Irish Belleek china, that "if you look real close, you can see the tiny fingerprints of the wee lassies that worked so hard to make it."

Sure that's a bit of blarney, but the point is very clear: Every piece of Belleek porcelain is fashioned by hand.

Belleek is also the most distinctive porcelain in the world: creamy white, with just a hint of pearly opalescence, silky to the touch, light as a feather, thin as an eggshell, and tough as nails.

The real story begins in the late 1850s, when, by the luck of the Irish, deposits of a special variety of kaolin, the rare china clay needed to make true porcelain, was discovered in the county of Fermanagh, Ireland.

Potters David Mc Burney and Robert Armstrong immediately started making decorative and utilitarian porcelain in the Fermanagh city of Belleek. They were soon joined by an English potter, William Bromley, who brought with him experienced workers from his pottery in Stoke-on-Trent, Staffordshire.

The earliest success for Belleek china was the introduction of hand-woven porcelain baskets decorated with tiny, hand-crafted leaves and flowers. Designed by William Henshal, these baskets became an instant hit, and they still are among the most sought after (and expensive) Belleek items on the antiques market.

Images of the sea, however, dominate most Belleek decoration—shells, seahorses, dolphins and coral, in particular. Then, of course, there is the symbolic Irish shamrock.

Most Belleek pieces are unpainted, relying for their beauty on appealing shapes and finely detailed embossed decoration. Shamrocks may be colored green, and some patterns are highlighted with a simple blush of pale green, yellow, coral or blue.

Belleek porcelain is still being made today, but those who collect usually only seek out the oldest pieces. These old pieces are also known as "black mark" Belleek, because that was the color of the first three stamps the company used to mark its wares.

The Belleek mark is a complicated one, incorporating the word Belleek, an Irish wolfhound, a harp, a tower and sprigs of shamrocks. The first black mark (1863-1890), while most often black, can also be found in red, green, blue and brown in very rare instances.

The second black mark (1891-1926) adds, underneath the name Belleek, a banner with the words "Co. Fermanagh Ireland." The third black mark (1926-46) adds, under that banner, a circular medallion with words in Gaelic and a registration number.

From 1946 up until 1980 the company used three different green marks and these days collectors have been picking up green-mark Belleek in antique shops, especially if the pieces are unusual, distinctively beautiful, or help the collector to complete a set. From 1980-92 the Belleek mark was gold/brown. The current mark is blue.

Belleek porcelain may have been lucky for the Irish, but by the late 19th Century it became lucky for America, too.

Old American Belleek currently has become even more highly sought after than the Irish variety. It was made in New Jersey, and it's quite an interesting story.

American Belleek: The Luck Of New Jersey

"Trenton Makes and the World Takes." That's the motto of the New Jersey state capital.

It's a slogan that was particularly appropriate at the turn of the last century, when manufacturers took advantage of the city's geographic proximity to the nation's two most lucrative markets: New York and Philadelphia.

One of the most famous and successful of those manufacturers was a man named Walter Lenox, and his is a remarkable story.

Lenox founded the Ceramic Art Company in Trenton in 1889 with Jonathan Coxon, Sr. He acquired sole ownership of the company in 1894, and Coxon left the company with more debts than assets in 1896. The company wouldn't be called Lenox until 1906.

One of Lenox's plans for saving the company included cashing in on the then current American craze for Irish Belleek china.

American buyers were suspicious at first, but Lenox hired some expert potters from the Belleek factories in Ireland, and with the marketing help of Harry A. Brown, the secretary of the company, he managed to place his version of Belleek wares in some of the finest shops, including the prestigious Shreve's in San Francisco.

The scuttlebutt had been that Lenox's Belleek was just not as sturdy as the Irish variety. But when a box of Lenox's shipment to Shreve's was unearthed, intact and unscathed, in the wreckage of the San Francisco earthquake, those rumors were put to rest for good.

With this proof of superior quality, Lenox began to achieve some real success, especially when he was able to add Tiffany's to his regular client list.

This success did not come easily for Lenox, however. He had been diagnosed with a disease that crippled his muscles and diminished his sight. Eventually he had to be carried piggyback by his chauffeur to his desk each day. Even when he had become quite blind, he continued to supervise every aspect of production, including inspecting the finished products by the feel of his sensitive fingers.

Lenox's hands-on control of the company paid off big in 1917, when President Woodrow Wilson, who had been governor of New Jersey, ordered a 1,700 piece set of dinnerware for the White House. It was the first American-made china for the White House, and the tradition continues to this day.

The White House set cost the taxpayers $16,000 dollars, a tidy sum in those days. For Lenox, however, the publicity from that sale would be priceless. In the years to follow, Lenox would get orders from governors' mansions across the nation and from foreign dignitaries as well.

Lenox died two years later in 1919. In his lifetime he had taken a bankrupt company to the pinnacle of success, and in so doing made quality American porcelain respectable around the world.

Collectors particularly love old Ceramic Art Company and early (green mark) Lenox pieces, especially those also marked as Belleek. Lenox ceased making Belleek china in 1930.

The China-Painting Craze (1895-1925)

Some of the most beautiful hand-painted porcelain ever produced was made right here in the United States during the Chicago china-painting craze that reached its height in the thirty years between 1895 to 1925.

The formula for this frenzy combined the Arts and Crafts Movement with the Women's Suffrage Movement. The storm was centered in Chicago, because that's where Susan Frackleton was.

In 1886, Frackleton wrote an enormously successful book, "Tried By Fire." It became the definitive work of the day on decorating porcelain for both amateurs and professionals. Her book inspired many women across the country to try their hand at painting ceramics. In a way, porcelain painting was an ideal way for women of all classes to express themselves artistically and to earn some independent income at the same time. Women who didn't need the income could engage in an enterprise unthreatening to their husbands, and women who really needed the extra money could avoid the drudgery of the sweatshops.

Frackleton was an ideal role model. As independent and enterprising as they come, she became something of a minor industry herself. Frackleton marketed a line of brushes, paints and china-decorating kits. She even offered the services of her kiln on the South Side of Chicago to those who didn't have the ovens necessary for firing their painted porcelains.

As the craze for painting china grew, groups of women formed clubs and studios, much in the manner of the Arts and Crafts guilds. To these Frackleton offered her "Frackleton Portable Gas-Kiln," specially designed so that the ladies, with the bulky, flouncy fashions of the day, would not set their clothes and themselves on fire.

Some of the wealthier women of the day were able to convince their husbands to invest in a china-decorating enterprise. One such woman was Pauline Jacobus, who founded Pauline Pottery in Chicago in 1882.

Pauline Jocobus was inspired by Maria Longworth Nichols, founder of Rookwood Pottery in Cincinnati, and Sarah Bernhardt, the famous actress who had exhibited some of her own decorated pottery at a local Chicago exhibition. Pauline's own decorated china became so much in demand that it was carried by such prestigious stores as Marshall Fields in Chicago and Tiffany in New York.

The most successful salesman for Pauline Pottery was a man named Wilder Pickard, who was responsible for about one-third of the pottery's total sales. Pickard was so successful that he and his wife Minnie started their own china-painting studio in Chicago in 1898.

Pickard would become the most prominent and long-lasting china-art studio in the United States. It is still in business today. Much of this china-decorating company's success had to do with its founder's instinct for marketing, but much more still was a result of the turn-of-the-century wave of immigration to the U.S. from central, southern and eastern Europe.

Pickard took advantage of this surge in immigration to supplement the usual amateur lady decorators with well-schooled male artists from Germany, Poland, Bohemia, Hungary and other European countries. The result was a line of the most exquisitely decorated china in the popular Art Nouveau style of the day—mostly stylized fruit and/or florals, heavily trimmed in gold.

You have to see these floral patterns to believe them. There is no more beautiful or accessible examples of hand-painted Art Nouveau decoration in the world.

No, it's not French Art Nouveau, not German or Austrian "Jungendstil." It's American Art Nouveau, and if you have a hard time believing it, I suggest you get yourself a copy of the "Collector's Encyclopedia of Pickard China: With Additional Sections on Other Chicago China Studios" by Alan B. Reed (Collector Books, 1995).

Pickard imported blank china from France, Germany and Japan, and bought blanks from Willets and the Ceramic Art Company (Lenox) in Trenton. But the paintings are very European. It is as if these immigrant artists wanted to prove themselves worthy of their new found land by bringing the best they could do to their work.

By 1916, there were 200 china-decorating studios in the United States, a great many of them in Chicago. By 1929 only fifteen of them had survived, including Pickard. The age of artful china in the United States was over, but not without leaving a breathtaking legacy. Pickard used various marks over the years, about nine different marks covering the years of their most artful production between 1900 and 1919. Some pieces will also be signed by the artist.

An Alphabet Soup Of Porcelains

This chapter promises to be a copy editor's nightmare, because it's all about German porcelains, a topic that can turn into something of an alphabet soup—too many letters, and long, unpronounceable names.

However, it is certainly a tasty soup. For nearly three centuries German porcelains have been consistently the best in the western world, and what the rest of Europe ever knew about porcelain it learned from the Germans.

It all began in January of 1708 in the city of Dresden with Johann Boettger, an alchemist in the employ of Augustus I, Elector of Saxony and King of Poland. Boettger unlocked the ancient Oriental secret for making a type of stoneware that was hard, white and shiny, and could be made as thin as an eggshell but still be tough as nails.

Two years later in Meissen, a suburb of Dresden, the first European porcelain factory was established. From that time on, the porcelains of Meissen and Dresden became the models for all European porcelain, not only in substance, but also in design and decoration.

When we talk of German porcelains, we mean the porcelains of Central Europe—Germany, Austria, Bohemia, Poland, Hungary, etc.—everywhere German porcelain manufacturers and artists had an influence.

Besides the factories of Dresden and Meissen, here are some other names to notice as signs of distinctive quality. Here is an alphabet worth remembering:

KPM. In German these initials stand for Royal Porcelain Manufacture. They were first used in Meissen around 1720, but were never protected by copyright. Meissen used the initials with a crossed-swords mark. But the best known uses of the KPM initials are either with a scepter, a single sword, a caduceus (sword and snake), an eagle, or an imperial orb. Those are the marks for the royal factory of Berlin, which was established in 1763 and dominated fine German porcelain manufacturing for the greater part of the 19th Century.

In the 20th Century, the initial KPM might have been used by any German manufacturer whose last name begins with a "K," like Krautzberger, Kranichfeld and Krister. These will have their own distinctive marks along with the initials, and while they are not Meissen or Berlin, they are still fine porcelains.

RS or ES. Reinhold and Erdmann Schlegelmilch began making porcelain in central Europe around 1861. Turn-of-the-century marks will include the initials of one of the brothers along with a factory site: Suhl, Saxe, Tillowitz, Poland or simply Germany.

It is the RS Prussia mark, however, that gets collectors so excited these days. That mark is the initials enshrined in a wreath and topped with a star.

RS Prussia pieces are distinctive for their irregular shapes (nothing is just round or square), which are identifiable even if a piece is unmarked. The rich decoration is evocative of its era—the opulent, Edwardian, Art Nouveau, Gilded Age—at the turn of the century.

ZS or ZSCR. These are the initials for the firm of Zeh, Scherzer & Co of Rehau, a city in Bavaria. Started in 1880, it is still in business.

HR. The initials for another fine Bavarian company, Hutschen-reuther, which began in 1814 and is also still in business.

R or RC. The Rosenthal Company, another Bavarian porcelain manufacturer still in business, was started in 1879. Pre-World War II pieces are preferred. A large scripted "R" stands for the city of Rudol-stadt.

OH or OHME. Hermann Ohme was best known for the turn-of-the-century pattern called "Old Ivory," which is highly collectible today. The company was in business from 1882 to 1930 in Nieder-slzbrunn, Silesia, which became the city of Szczawienko in Poland.

CT. Carl Tielsch began his company in Altwasser, Silesia in 1845, and it is still in business in the Polish city of Walbrzych. It is probably best known for those highly decorative dishes—two bowls joined by a center handle—called lobster dishes.

OS. Oscar Schaller began making fine porcelain dinnerware and figurines in Windischeschenbach, Germany in 1918, and is still in business.

CS or S&C. Carl Schumann & Compay started making fine porcelain dinnerware in Arzberg, Bavaria, in 1896, and is still in business.

MZ. You may see Moritz Zdekauer's porcelains marked either Bohemia, Austria or Czechoslovakia. The company was in business from 1884 to 1945 in the city of Altrohlau, which became the modern city of Stara.

HC. Of all types of German porcelain, hand-painted bisque (unglazed porcelain) figurines are now quite the rage, and Heubach Brothers made many of them. They are probably best known for their doll heads and for the popularly collectible "piano babies," figurines of infants that were used to keep the piano shawl from slipping off the piano. The company was started in Lichte, Thuringia, and is still in business.

These are just some of the more commonly found German porcelain companies to use initials in their marks. They are by no means the end of the story in German porcelains. Other fine companies to look for include Royal Bonn, Royal Austria and Hungary's Herend porcelain.

What's My China?

It's time once again to play "What's My China?"

As a TV game show host, I'll have to let people call me Art (Ugh), but that's show biz. Anyone who can stump me will win the home version of "What's My China," as soon as I figure out what that is. Anyway, bring on the first contestant!

Art, my dishes are marked "The Limoges China Company," then they say "Made in USA." I thought Limoges china was made in France. So, Art, what's my china?

That's an easy one. The Limoges China Company began in Sebring, Ohio in 1904. After World War II, the company changed the name to the American Limoges China Company, because it was sued by the Chamber of Commerce of the real porcelain-producing city of Limoges in France.

American Limoges dishes are collectible in their own right, but many of the transfer patterns, particularly the florals, are rather dowdy and not up to the standards of hand-painted French Limoges dishes. The company bought many of its china transfer patterns from Germany, and pieces decorated with these have become as collectible as the German pieces.

Most collectible in American Limoges are fish and game patterns, patterns featuring monks, portraits or fruit motifs, and children's dishes. The company went out of business in 1958.

Bring on the next contestant.

Art, I inherited some pretty dishes with flowers all over them. On the bottom of the dishes it's says they were made in England by James Kent and there is a pattern name "Du Barry." But I recently saw a plate like mine in an antique shop for over $100, and the tag called it "Chintz." A hundred dollars doesn't sound chintzy to me. So, Art, what's my china?

Your china is a style of English china nicknamed "Chintz." The name comes from the Hindi word "chint," a cotton fabric, painted or stained in a floral design. Importers in the mid-1700s referred to a cargo of chints (plural), so the plural became the singular, spelled chintz, so now the plural is chintzes. So much for the grammar lesson.

Chintz fabrics were painted in no less than five colors and they were less expensive than woven fabrics, so some people considered them gaudy and cheap. Thus the word "chintzy."

English Chintz ceramics were first produced beginning around 1910 and continuously through the 1950s in the city of Stoke on Trent, England, which includes the towns of Burslem, Hanley, Longton and Tunstall. Several English companies made Chintz patterns in bone china, earthenware and semi-porcelain under scores of different pattern names.

Well, no one's won the big prize yet, so bring on the next contestant.

Some people say hand-painted dishes are more valuable, but I can't tell whether mine are hand-painted or not, Art. What's my china?

Now I know something I can include in the home version of this game—a high-powered magnifying glass or a jeweler's loupe. That's so you can look closely at the decoration to see if you can find those tiny dot patterns that are part of a printed transfer-decal. Otherwise you should see the brush stokes from hand-painting. Some dishes were decorated with a combination of transfer prints and hand-painting.

While it's generally accepted that hand-painted plates are more desirable, they are not always more valuable. Consider that you can pay $100 or more for an early English transfer plate, while a hand-painted dinner plate from Limoges might only cost $25 to $50. Next!

Art, my dishes have no identifying marks underneath, but some of them have numbers impressed on the bottom and others have weird squiggly lines impressed. So, what's my china?

It's not a hard-and-fast rule, but impressed numbers, especially in a series of four, sometimes accompanied with two other numbers elsewhere on the bottom, usually indicate the piece was made in Germany. Impressed squiggly lines may indicate the piece was made in France, either in Sevres or Paris. Handwritten numbers or letters on porcelain could be English artist's marks. Printed numbers, stamped on the bottom of a piece, mean it was most likely made in Japan.

These are just clues to identifying your china. You have to also consider the quality of the clay and the style of decoration.

Well, that's all the time we have for "What's My China?" today—or any day, unfortunately. My producers tell me that to compete on TV, I'll have to play future editions of "What's My China?" with male strippers, unfaithful husbands, or teenage daughters who dress like tramps.

It's enough letting people call me Art.

All's Well That Ends Up Weller

Like many of the stories about American pottery, the story of Weller pottery is a classic American success story.

In 1872 Sam Weller opened his own pottery business in Fultonham, Ohio. His "factory" consisted of a small log cabin, a grinding machine, one kiln (pottery oven) and a wagon. The "staff" included himself, his assistant, Summer Fauley, and an old white horse.

Their operation ran this way:

The horse brought a wagon-load of clay to the cabin and propelled the grinding machine that processed the clay. Weller and Fauley fashioned, glazed and fired the pots. Then the horse hauled the finished products just outside of town. The town was Zanesville, Ohio.

Weller had been a craftsman in the Ohio sewer tile business, but felt he was destined for better things.

So when his horse and wagon-load of wares approached the outskirts of town, he had Fauley stay with it while he dressed in his finest clothes. With an air of utmost confidence and suavity, he rode a streetcar into town to call upon its most prosperous merchants.

Weller was hardly an overnight success. He and Fauley worked the operation this way for ten years, increasing their client list and their variety of wares, which now included flower pots, crocks, cuspidors and vases.

When success did come, it came quickly. Competing merchants began clamoring for Weller's wares.

In 1882 the company moved to a bigger space in Zanesville, Ohio, and acquired a larger warehouse in 1888. By 1890 he had moved to an even larger location employing 68 men and increased production to include ornamental flower baskets, jardinieres and umbrella stands.

Weller had become a force to be reckoned with in the American pottery business. By the turn of the century, his company would have nearly 500 employees.

In 1904, thirty-four years after he began his one-horse operation, he would achieve the pinnacle of success—winning a gold medal at the St. Louis World's Fair for "The World's Largest Vase," a seven-foot wonder of beautifully decorated pottery in a glossy glaze he called "Aurelian" for its golden luster.

Weller had come a long way from the little log cabin with the horse—a bona fide American success story. He repaid the city of Zanesville in 1903 by building a magnificent theater—tiled, decorated and detailed with Weller pottery, of course—which became so renown for its beauty and acoustical excellence that it attracted actors and performers from all over the world.

Sam Weller died in October of 1925. The Weller Pottery Company ceased operations in 1948. And the Weller Theater closed down in 1958.

Weller's legacy and the source of his success—his incredibly varied array of beautiful art pottery—is now highly sought after on the antique market. Smart collectors long ago realized that America just doesn't make pottery anymore, at least not like it used to, and certainly not as evocative of its time as Weller's. That's why the market for old American ceramics from the 1860s to the 1960s is so exciting.

The Inventive Messrs. Wedgwood

Certain well-known names just seem to merit a special cachet of excellence.

The field of British ceramics is crowded with special names: Minton, Spode, Worcester, Derby, Doulton, Coalport, and Shelley, just to mention a few. In the public eye, however, one name leads the pack—Wedgwood.

There were actually two Messrs. Wedgwood, Josiah I and II, and here's the story why they so richly deserve their popular acclaim:

Because of its rich clay deposits, the county of Staffordshire became England's pottery center early on. Most wares were utilitarian, crude and made mostly for the local and national market inside Britain.

By the early 1700s, however, Staffordshire potters started losing some of their market to imports. The Dutch, who dominated trade with the Orient, began to use the techniques they learned from the Chinese in their pottery center in Delft. Then, there was the direct impact of Chinese imports themselves. The Germans finally developed a European porcelain in Dresden in 1708, and were exporting it from their factory in that city's suburb of Meissen.

Josiah Wedgwood believed the best way to beat this formidable competition was to meet it head-on by boldly experimenting with Staffordshire's most abundant resource, the clay itself. By developing compelling new forms and interesting new colors and glazes, he kept the public's interest piqued and before long, Staffordshire potters not only had captured their home market, but were exporting to foreign countries as well.

Wedgwood was born in the northern Staffordshire city of Burslem and as a teenager was an apprentice in pottery-making to his father, Thomas. In 1759 he started his own business in that city and by 1762 he had interested Queen Charlotte in an experimental dinnerware, a creamy white, porcelain-like ware, which he named "Queensware" in her honor.

Wedgwood moved to a new Staffordshire factory in 1769. He called the place "Etruria," for the ancient Etruscan-style art vases he first produced there to commemorate the move. It was in the Etruria factory, in 1774, that Wedgwood produced the ware that would be his trademark into the 20th Century—Jasperware.

Jasperware is a thin, fine stoneware that feels rough to the touch like the bisque (unglazed) porcelain it was meant to compete with. The name comes from jasper, a metallic oxide dye created during the Renaissance. Wedgwood stained his wares in an array of colors: cobalt blue, green, maroon, lilac, yellow, black, white, and the light blue that became so famous it is known to this day as "Wedgwood blue." The outside of the pieces are decorated with classical figures, sculpted from life, and applied in cameo-like relief.

Josiah died in 1795, but his son, Josiah II, continued the company's policy of competing by experimentation and innovation. His most significant contribution came in 1830 with his formula to blur and smear the glaze on blue and white, decal-decorated transferware to make his stoneware look more like hand-painted Oriental porcelain.

Today these wares are called "flow blue," but for the next 80 years, until the outbreak of World War I, it would be the midline, middle-class, everyday dinnerware throughout Great Britain and the United States.

Flow blue was so successful, it was produced by over 200 different potteries in nearly 2,000 different patterns from 1830 until around 1910.

Here are just some of the Wedgewood company's experimental wares that captured the rich Victorian market in the 19th Century, and the hearts of today's collectors:

Pearlware (cobalt oxide acts like laundry bluing to produce a lustrous white-ware), Caneware (a pale buff stoneware), rosso antico (a glaze from red to chocolate brown), Drabware (an olive-gray pottery loved by Victorians), and Fairyland Luster (decorated with gothic figures and landscapes in a lustrous, metalic glaze).

An innovator such as Wedgwood is bound to have imitators. Collectors know that if it isn't marked Wedgwood, it probably isn't Wedgwood.

Look for Wedgwood wares whenever you go antiquing. Like most of the finest antiques, they are truly evocative of their times. They deserve the prestige rating that they have, because they represent an inspirational spirit of bold competitiveness, intelligent science, and imaginative artistry that we can't help but admire.

The Answer Is Spode

If you haven't got a clue about why old English dinnerware is so popular these days, here's a few clues you might find for a five-letter word in the N.Y. *Times* crossword puzzles: "Fine china," "Elegant dinnerware," "Early English ceramic artist," or "Formal table service."

The answer to all these clues is "SPODE," a name that even the puzzle-makers know to be synonymous with the best of old English dinnerware, and a major reason why it is so sought-after on today's antiques market.

Why is Spode always the answer? Well, here are just three reasons that should cinch it for you:

1. Spode perfected the under-glaze transfer pattern technique that became the basis for all successful Staffordshire wares;

2. It is Spode's "Blue Willow" pattern, called "True Willow" to this day, that became one of the most enduring English dinnerware patterns ever produced; and

3. Spode invented bone china, one of the most beautiful and collectible porcelain-like substances ever made.

Josiah Spode I, after working in the Staffordshire pottery industry for many years, started his own business in Stoke on Trent around

1770. In 1778, he opened a London showroom and staffed it with his son, Josiah II.

Josiah I died in 1787, leaving his son a formula for making a porcelain ware from calcined ox bones. Ox bones had been burned to produce a black ink. But Spode discovered that when the bones were twice-burned they became a white ash that could be used to make a substance as thin and white and hard as the finest eggshell porcelain.

Josiah II perfected his father's formula and was marketing fine bone china by the year 1800.

English potters had long been seeking a way to compete with imported Chinese wares and Spode was in the forefront. In 1810 he developed three different "Blue Willow" patterns, based on Chinese Nanking wares. The last of these became known as "True Willow," the pattern that has been passed down to us today. That pattern became so popular, by 1830 two hundred Staffordshire potters were imitating it.

Spode's next contribution came in 1814. "New Stone," as it was called, looked exactly like the old gray-white Chinese porcelain wares and with hand-painted and gilt decoration, it became one of the most popular English tablewares of the pre-Victorian era.

Spode's contributions to the craze for English Romantic transferware scenes came in 1814 with "Tower" and 1816 with "Italian." Both of these strikingly beautiful dark blue patterns are still hotly collected today.

When Josiah I died back in 1787, Josiah II went to work at the Stoke factory and put William Copeland in charge of the London showroom. But Copeland died in 1827 and Josiah II a few years later, leaving the company in the hands of Copeland's son, W. T. Copeland.

In 1833, W. T. brought in Thomas Garrett as a partner and the firm's name was changed to Copeland & Garrett until 1847. From then until 1970 marks on the backs of the company's wares read either just "Copeland" or "Copeland-Spode."

Copeland didn't just maintain the high quality dinnerware the company had become known for. In 1842, he introduced a remarkable statuary ware called "Parian," a bisque (unglazed) porcelain polished to look like marble.

From large sculptures to busts and statuettes, Copeland's Parian was heavily produced and widely imitated until the outbreak of World War I in 1914.

Parian was so enormously popular in its time, that it is hard to call any authentic Victorian or Edwardian decor complete today without some Parian statuary ware in evidence.

In 1970 the company was renamed simply "Spode," as a tribute to the father and son who started it all two centuries before.

So, What's That Jug Made Of?

The story goes that once upon a time, a long, long time ago, a legendary drunkard named Toby Fillpot sat drinking and smoking his pipe under the shade of a tree, and died there full and happy.

Toby's legend was put to song in 1761 by the English minister, Rev. Francis Fawkes, in the song "Little Brown Jug." The jug in the song, according to the lyrics of the first stanza,

"… was once Toby Fillpott, a thirsty old soul,

As e'er drank a bottle or fathom'd a bowl;

In boozing about 'twas his praise to excel,

And among the jolly topers he bore off the bell."

Notice the words don't say the jug *belonged* to Toby Fillpot; it *was* Toby Fillpot!

The poem explains that several years after Toby passed on to that great pub in the sky,

"His body, when long in the ground it had lain,

And time into clay had resolved it again."

So, a local potter took that clay,

"And with part of fat Toby he form'd this brown jug."

Since the time the Rev. Fawkes wrote his song, the "Toby" jug, formed to resemble that loveable old sot, has been the most recognizable of all English jugs. But the first Toby jug may have been the invention of (Egad!) a Frenchman. His name was Jean Voyez, and he was something of a legend himself.

Voyez was an artist who worked in Staffordshire sculpting from life those white classical figures that appear in relief on pieces of Wedgwood's famous jasperware. He had a reputation as a drinker and philanderer, which the straight-laced Wedgwood overlooked in deference to the man's enormous talent.

One day, however, Wedgwood entered the sculpting studio unannounced to discover Voyez and a nude model, both drunk and in a compromising position. (Can we ever look at those classical ladies the same?)

Wedgwood had Voyez arrested and he spent three months in jail for fornication. On his release, Voyez vowed revenge. He immediately went to work for one of Wedgwood's competitors, Ralph Wood. Not long later, Wood and Voyez produced the first Toby jugs.

Now Wedgwood, who was always the innovator, was forced to become a copier, as he and other Staffordshire potters scrambled to cash in on the huge popularity of the Voyez-Wood jugs.

We call them pitchers, but the British call them jugs, and jug collecting is a British tradition that goes back to the Middle Ages, way before that first Toby jug. Author and collector James Paton explained the popularity of jugs best in his book, "Jugs, a Collector's Guide" (Souvenir Press):

"Of all the familiar articles man has manufactured to improve his life, to civilize it, the jug is for me the most important. The cup, the drinking mug, the tankard, these are personal objects. But the jug is communal, something to be shared, a symbol of friendship."

The medieval practice of decorating with jugs returned during the Gothic Revival of the Victorian era. Today's collectors collect these as well as the revived Toby jugs developed for Royal Doulton by Charles Noke in 1933 and which are still produced today.

Romancing The Stoneware

From a simple shard of a clay pot, archaeologists have been able to tell us a great deal about an entire civilization. Ceramics seem to have the magic to evoke the times in which they were made more than anything else produced during the same period.

This is because ceramics touch ordinary people in their everyday lives—their daily routine, how and what they eat, how food is prepared and stored. Ceramics can also offer an insight into cosmetic use, religious observances and funerary practices.

Because ceramics can break, they are constantly being produced, and this production can offer clues about a society's manufacturing capabilities and economic conditions as well as the kinds of colors and decorations they preferred.

All of this holds true not only for ancient ceramics, but also for the ceramic items available on today's antiques market, and in few places is it more evident than in the Romantic transferwares produced in Staffordshire, England during the 19th Century (ca.1820-ca.1870)

In England a shire is what we call a county, and the county of Staffordshire began developing as a pottery center during the 18th Century. By the middle of the 19th Century, there were over 130 pottery manufacturers at work in the shire's various cities—Longton, Burslem,

Stoke on Trent, Hanley, etc.—producing two-thirds of all the pottery made in England.

One of the reasons for Staffordshire's success was the potters' use of a technique for transferring prints onto their wares. The use of prints meant that wares could be more quickly and cheaply mass-produced than items that required hand-painting by professional artists.

Transfer printing also meant that wares could be decorated with elaborately detailed decorations, and that all the pieces in even the most extensive table service would match.

As it happens, around the year 1800 a clergyman, William Gilpin, toured rural England and published his writings and illustrations. The idyllic scenery in his prints struck a nostalgic note among the citizens of Britain's gritty cities and industrial towns.

Soon publishers were scrambling to produce illustrated travel books, and Staffordshire's potters began decorating their tablewares and chamber sets with the same kind of scenery.

The Romantic designs on Staffordshire pottery include scenes of foreign and exotic places, rural and pastoral scenes, nostalgic scenes of domestic bliss, Gothic castles, gardens and landscapes, sporting scenes, and dense decorations of birds, animals, fruits and flowers.

The titles of these scenes, often printed on the underside of the dishes, indicate just what kind of Romantic escapism was the taste of the day—Andalusia, Caledonia, Athens, Palestine, Persia, Spanish

Convent, Cyprus, Bird of Paradise, Gypsies, Sheltered Peasants, Italian Buildings, Boy Piping, Botanical Beauties, Asiatic Plants, etc.

Romantic Staffordshire transfers were produced on earthenware up until the 1830s, on stoneware up through the early 1850s, and then on semi-porcelain after that. Scenes were produced in various shades of blue, green, pink, lavender, mulberry (a gray-red-brown), brown, black, and in various polychrome combinations.

Whatever the color, however, it's the scenes on these dishes that captivate us. Stare at them long enough, and you'll want to walk right into them and be a part of their world.

Willowware: An Opera
On A Plate

Blue Willow dinnerware has been collected since it first appeared in England nearly 200 years ago. It has long been a standard stock-in-trade for the antique business on every level from rural yard sales to New York's high-powered Park Avenue Armory Show.

Back in the 18th Century (1700s), European potters were frantically looking for ways to compete with the popularity of Chinese blue and white export wares. In Germany the answer would be Meissen's "Blue Onion" pattern. For the Dutch it would be blue and white patterns from Delft. The first English response would be Willow.

The earliest design of an English Willow pattern is generally ascribed to Thomas Turner, an artist with the Caughley factory, in 1780. Thomas Minton produce a pattern in 1790 called "Willow Nanking," after the popular blue and white wares exported from that Chinese city.

About this time, the Spode factories in Staffordshire were starting to produce the first of what would be three different Willow patterns. The third of these, "Willow III," was introduced in 1810, and is called "True Willow," because it is the standard for the recognizable pattern that comes down to us today.

The Spode Willow pattern includes an outer border of geometric designs and scrolled cartouches, and an inner border of diamond-shaped geometrics. The center of the pattern features a scene of such mystery and complexity that it's been the subject of stories and legends for two centuries.

The basic elements of this scene consist of the following: To the right are two buildings, presumably a teahouse and a pavilion, and next to these is a fruit tree, an apple or orange, impossibly bearing both fruit and blossoms at the same time, a clue that whatever story is here is a fiction, a fairy tale.

Slightly off center is the willow tree that dominates the scene. To the left is a bridge, usually with three arches underneath, and on the bridge there are three people, who look like they are carrying lanterns. On the left is a man rowing a boat, and on the upper left is an island with an Oriental-style building on it, presumably a temple.

At the top center of the pattern two turtle doves face each other with their wings outstretched in flight. At the bottom of the pattern a zigzagging fence separates us from the scene like the proscenium of a stage. These characters seem to be trapped in this drama.

The legend of the Blue Willow scene, in all its variations, is basically a Romeo and Juliet-style story of tragic love. A young girl (Hon Shee, Koong-shee or Lichi) falls in love with a young man (usually called Chang). The girl's wealthy father, however, has arranged a marriage he feels would be better suited to his daughter's station in life.

So, the young lovers run away only to die—depending on the legend—by either murder, heartbreak or drowning. The turtle doves represent their reunion in the afterlife, and the willow weeps at the tragic tale.

The stories associated with the Willow pattern simply developed over time. They have nothing to do with any traditional Chinese legends, nor were they conceived by the original designers, manufacturers or marketers of the wares.

Aside from the basic elements of the pattern, not all Willowware looks alike. There are at least nine different border variations and ten different variations in the scene. Some have butterflies, insects or florals on the border. Some have only one or two people on the bridge. Some have no bridge at all. There are more or fewer buildings in other variations. And besides blue, the pattern was also made in pink, green and polychrome (multi-colors), sometimes called "Gaudy Willow."

The price of Willowware varies with the quality, age and collectors' demand. Some of the best Staffordshire Willowwares are by such companies as Spode, Allertons, Ridgways, Clews, Adams, Meakin, Ashworth, Wood, and Booths. The most sought-after American Blue Willow is turn-of-the-century Buffalo Pottery.

Over the years, Willowware has been so popular that all sorts of items were made in the pattern. Look for such Willow rarities as inkwells, lamp bases, clocks, perfume bottles and even toasters.

There is also Willow glassware, cocktail sets, tablecloths, napkins, place mats, flatware, serving utensils, enamel cookware, notepaper, and decals and stencils for decorating furniture.

You might not want to get that carried away. But Blue Willow is charming, warm, romantic and stately, a practical and perfectly respectable alternative to high-priced flow blue and other Staffordshire blue and white pottery.

Looking For Mr. Wright

In 1947, when New York's Gimbel's department store ran a small ad for Russel Wright's "American Modern" dinnerware, a line formed around the block the next morning and several people were injured in the stampede as the store opened.

This incident at Gimbel's forever changed the way fine department stores did business. Previously, a customer chose an item from the floor display and placed an order with a salesman, who then called down to the stockroom to have it brought up.

On that particular sale day, however, salesmen were rushed by hundreds of customers, and they wrote up orders without the stock to back them up. So, Gimbel's decided to put the stock right out on the floor for customers to pick up, supermarket style, as it's done today.

When Wright had presented the American Modern line to Steubenville Pottery in the late 1930s, the company balked at first. The sweeping futuristic shapes were considered much too radical. And when the line was first introduced in 1939, sales were initially slow.

But post-war America was finally ready for modern American designer dinnerware, and sales of American Modern zoomed. By 1951, Steubenville was producing 12 million pieces a year, and over 80 million pieces would be produced before the line was discontinued in 1959.

This success also made Russel Wright a household name. After a while, department stores would take out large ads where the name Russel Wright, which was not a brand name, would dominate, printed in larger type than even the name of the store itself.

American Modern was made in original colors of White, Bean Brown, Chartreuse, Coral (a pink), Curry, Sea Foam (a green-blue), and a Granite Grey, which Wright considered the most flattering color for food display. In 1950, the Bean Brown was replaced with Black Chutney and Cedar Green was added.

Quaker-born Wright was quite the serious artist and a superb marketer of his wares. He directed advertisements of American Modern to young married couples who were just starting a home together, and he made his dinnerware affordable, while maintaining an elegant and classy appeal.

Even today American Modern pieces are affordable because they are available in such quantity. But serving pieces like pitchers and teapots can get expensive in rare colors.

Wright's "Casual" china dinnerware for Iroquois Pottery, introduced in 1946, is harder to find and can be a bit pricier than American Modern.

Some colors are more desirable in Wright's patterns. In American Modern, "Sea Foam" always gets more money. In the Casual pattern, the Oyster and Charcoal colors can get up to 50-percent more.

Wright also designed dinnerware for Harker, Bauer, Knowles and Ideal, as well as items in spun aluminum, glass and sterling silver. His ceramic kitchen clock, designed for Harker, is particularly neat.

PART IV
Stories About Glass

The Ingenious Origins Of Glass * American Brilliance * The Unsinkable C. F. Monroe * L.C. Tiffany: Beauty And The Best * Victor Durand: A Tiffany for New Jersey * The Truth About Loetz * The Art Glass of Bohemia * Good Scents Collecting * Pressed Pattern Glass * Opal, Opaline, Opalescent * How To Speak Italian Glass * New Prosperity for Depression Glass * The Multiple Personalities of Steuben Glass

The Ingenious Origins Of Glass

As the legend is told, about 5,000 years ago some merchant sailors from Syria (then, Phoenicia) took refuge from a storm on a small island in the eastern Mediterranean. They were on their way home from Egypt with a valuable cargo of freshly mined soda. We call the stuff sodium carbonate or natron, and it was used for a variety of purposes from curing meats to curing upset stomachs. It was so highly prized that it could be traded as currency.

To warm themselves and dry their clothing, the sailors built roaring fires on the beach. They managed to support their cooking pots over the huge flames by using slabs of the soda, which had come from the mines—at great cost in human labor—in bulky chunks, hard, shiny and porous.

When the Syrian sailors awoke the next morning, they found the beach strewn with glittering jewels. During the night, the unusually hot fires had melted the blocks of soda, fusing them with the sand and ashes. The result was a wonderful new substance—glass.

The story is probably not true. Those fires could never have been hot enough to produce glass. But the place of glass's origin, the Middle East, is most likely correct. And the point of the legend is clear: wonderful things can happen when you combine thriving commerce, hard work, human ingenuity and luck.

We don't know who first found the formula for glass, but we do know who started the American glass industry, and he was something of an ingenious fellow himself. His name was Caspar Wistar.

Although there had been attempts at making glass on this continent as early as the first settlement in Jamestown, Wistar was the first to succeed. His rags-to-riches story combines all the ingredients of the old legend with all the trappings of the American Dream.

An immigrant from Baden, Germany, Wistar wasn't exactly penniless when he landed in Philadelphia in September of 1717. He had nine cents. He spent five on a loaf of bread and three to pay off a debt. So, with one penny in his pocket, he went to work hauling ashes on the docks.

Somehow he found a job with a maker of brass buttons and learned the trade well. Soon Wistar was teaching his son, Richard. Then he opened his own business making "Philadelphia buttons," which became so popular in those zipperless days that they were sold under that name in New York and Boston advertised as "renowned for their durability."

Wistar's success gave him the money to speculate, and an investment in glass making, although risky, must have seemed smart. It was risky because the royal governors were supposed to encourage imports to the colonies from England, taxed imports, like glass. But in 1739, Wistar established his glassworks in the town of Alloway in Salem county, New Jersey.

He lured glassmakers from Germany with the promise of unlimited opportunity. He built homes for himself and his workers and called the village Wistarburg. And so, a once nearly penniless immigrant took one of the earliest rebellious steps toward this country's economic independence.

The glassworks at Wistarburg produced mostly commercial bottles, scientific glass (Ben Franklin used some), and windowpanes. Workers produced table glass for themselves and for local consumption. They used the same formula as for windows and bottles, creating a "South Jersey"-style tableware, crude but often fancifully decorated with applied and tooled ornament.

Wistar won the legal battles to keep his plant in operation but it wouldn't outlast the Revolutionary War. It closed in 1777. Wistar, however, lived to see his adopted country free. He died in 1780.

Wistar's bold enterprise eventually established New Jersey as the glass capital of the nation. He laid the groundwork for an industry that would flourish well into the 20th Century. New Jersey, particularly South Jersey, became synonymous with American glass, and was even celebrated in poetry, as in these lines by Carl Sandberg:

"Down in southern New Jersey, they make glass. By day and by night, The fires burn on in Millville, and bid the sand let in the light."

American Brilliance

At the 1876 American Centennial Exhibition in Philadelphia, U.S. glassmakers stunned the world with the introduction of their "Brilliant Cut Glass," a heavy, crystal-clear glass, 48-percent lead, with hundreds of impossibly deep, sharp cuts in fancy geometric patterns that caught the light and made it dance.

Many of us own pieces of Brilliant Cut that survived to be passed down to us. If you do not, check out a piece at your local antique shop and observe the deepest, sharpest cut in it. That's called the "miter cut," the first cut made in the glass by a craftsman called the "rougher."

The cuts that fill in the miter cut design are called "motif cuts." They are made by specialists called "smoothers." Some smoothers specialized in diamonds, others in stars, pinwheels, hobnails, sunbursts, etc. Other smoothers cut notches on handles or points on rims.

I have seen photographs of the workshops where American Brilliant glass was made. It's quite a production. Long tables are set under an elaborate pulley system, from which hang cutting tools resembling old-fashioned dentists' drills. Along these tables, scores of highly skilled glass cutters work at their various specialties, then hand the glass down the line to the next craftsman. It's fairly obvious that this was a very expensive and labor-intensive process. It might take as many as ten men to make a fruit bowl. But the results were dazzling.

Not long after the turn of the century, however, glass companies started looking for ways to cut labor costs. Some, like Sinclair in Corning, New York, developed copper-wheel engraving in 1908. Using the same heavy crystal, fewer artists made shallower cuts in artful designs.

By 1910, most companies began producing a "gravic"-style glass, where heavy crystal was shallow cut in realistic designs like leaves and flowers. By 1917, when America entered World War I and workers were scarce, Brilliant Cut glass disappeared for good.

Most Brilliant Cut was not signed, so those pieces that are will be considered choice, especially if they are from one of several highly respected companies like Hawkes, Dorflinger, Sinclair, Clark, Libbey, among others.

Cherish the American Brilliant that was handed down to you, or consider collecting it. It's really beautiful stuff, and owning and passing it down to the next generation is, well, something of a patriotic duty.

The Unsinkable C. F. Monroe

"The sun was beating down on my head with not a breath of wind stirring, and a heavy swell rolling from the sea.... The sleeves of my shirt had shrunk from the wrist to the elbows and my hands and arms and face were blistered from exposure to the sun.... One eye was entirely closed and the other ran. Where blisters had peeled off, my arms were raw and bleeding and the salt water had hardly made them feel better, but I kept straight on."

In 1876, the year of the American centennial, Charles Fabian Monroe decided to take up a challenge. At only 20 years old and, by his own account, a wiry 127 pounds, he set out to row a canoe from New Bedford, Massachusetts to Philadelphia, a distance of 430 miles. He built the canoe himself and called it the *M. Eugenie.* The quote above is from a newspaper account he gave of the last miles of his journey.

Monroe became something of a celebrity that year. Steamships had followed him on his voyage and reported his progress. Crowds had lined the shores to catch a glimpse and cheer as he passed. For four days after his arrival in Philadelphia he was the guest of honor at ceremonies and receptions as a symbol of youthful America's rugged individualism.

And what did this tough young daredevil do for a living? He was a glass decorator.

At the time of his excursion, Monroe worked for the New England Glass Company of New Bedford. He had already traveled abroad to study design and decorative techniques. Four years later, in 1880, Monroe opened his own decorating studio in Meriden, Connecticut. Still only in his twenties, and working as a designer for the Meriden Flint Glass Company, Monroe retailed local glass, some decorated by himself, along with imported items that folks would have to travel to New York or Boston to get.

From the description of Monroe's shop, published in the *Meriden Daily Republican* in 1882, business was booming, perhaps in no small measure due to his hard-won celebrity. There were Belgian carpets and damask curtains, Victorian walnut furniture and brass chandeliers. Monroe expanded his line to include original oil paintings, porcelain figurines, bronze statuary, and the artful metal craft of another famous Meriden company, Bradley and Hubbard.

By 1892, Monroe had expanded his glass decorating business and was employing 200 designers, decorators and craftsmen. And on October 4 of that year, after officially incorporating his business, he patented the line of glass that would make him really famous, and become one of today's most sought-after collectibles.

Monroe called the line "Wave Crest," probably after the "heavy swell rolling from the sea" he had conquered sixteen years earlier. Called "opal ware," it's an acid-washed, satin milk glass that resembles porcelain. Monroe purchased the glass from companies like Mt. Washington—Pairpoint in New Bedford and Roedefer in Bel Air, Ohio.

Monroe and his artists decorated the glass with backgrounds in pink, green, blues or yellows and fired them onto the piece. Various motifs, mostly florals, were then painted on with acid-reduced enamels, and the piece was fired again. Finally, raised decoration—beading, scrolling and threading—was applied in white, colorful enamels and gilt. The effect can be breathtakingly beautiful.

The Wave Crest line included boxes for jewelry, powder, cuffs, collars, handkerchiefs and cigars. Pieces often had brass feet, collars and hinges. Vases were trimmed with gilt brass collars and handles.

In 1904 Monroe patented another line called "Kelva" with a marbleized background. Before he sold his business in 1916, he also produced "Nakara," a line of oriental-style wares.

During the 24-year period of Monroe's remarkable production, he was constantly faced with heavy competition from European and Oriental imports. If there is a moral to the C. F. Monroe story, it's in what he learned at sea when he was 20 years old: the best way to respond to any challenge is to try a bit harder to go a bit farther.

L.C. Tiffany: Beauty And The Best

Here's what Louis Comfort Tiffany (1848–1933) said at a celebration of his sixty-eighth birthday in 1916:

"If I may be forgiven a word about my own work, I would merely say that I have always striven to fix beauty in wood or stone or glass or pottery, in oil or water color, by using whatever seemed fittest for the expression of beauty; that has been my creed ... "

Few people so fully achieve what they strive for in life as successfully as Tiffany did.

L.C. Tiffany was the son of Charles Lewis Tiffany (1812-1902), founder of the famous Tiffany & Co. jewelry store in New York City in 1837.

A handsome and well-to-do young man, he might simply have stayed in the family business. Instead, he embarked on a remarkable career in art and design that would make the name Tiffany synonymous with the best that money could buy.

This reputation was hard won. First, Tiffany studied art with great masters. He traveled abroad to Europe and North Africa and documented his travels in oil and watercolors.

In 1875 he returned to America and started L.C. Tiffany & Associated Artists. While in Europe he had become fascinated by the stained glass windows of the great gothic cathedrals. Now he made them for people like Cornelius Vanderbilt, Mark Twain and President Chester Arthur, as well as scores of churches, universities, public buildings and private homes around the country.

But his business wasn't all about windows. To pursue his goal of creating "good art for American homes," he began making his trademark Tiffany lamps so everyone could have stained glass in the home.

Tiffany was very much a part of the burgeoning Art Nouveau Movement of his times. His windows and lamp shades would become typical of that organic style's playfulness with light, color and movement. They celebrate these things in nature—wisteria, dragonflies, spider webs, dogwood blossoms (a Japanese influence), peacock feathers and peonies (a Chinese influence).

In 1880, at the age of thirty-two, he became the youngest member inducted into the National Academy of Design. But he didn't rest on those laurels.

The next year, 1881, he started the Tiffany Glass Co. in Corona, Queens, with the English glass artist, Arthur Nash. There they developed what they would call "Favrille" glass from a medieval word meaning handmade.

Favrille is an iridescent glass with a slick metallic surface that shimmers green gold, blue and purple. It was widely imitated from the beginning by art glass houses like Johann Loetz, and by the mass-producers of carnival glass that would become known as "the poor man's Tiffany glass."

The point of Favrille was that all the artistry was done at the furnace by the glass artist. No decoration was applied afterwards. You'll find no Tiffany glass that is gilt or enameled.

Favrille was a big hit at the Paris Exhibition of 1900, as were many other Tiffany creations. He won several medals and citations and became world-renowned. Still, he wasn't stopping there.

That same year, he started yet another company, Tiffany Studios, where he would produce, among other things, desk sets and vanity sets in silver, bronze and bronze d'ore (gold-plated bronze).

When his father died in 1902, Louis Comfort took over the family jewelry business in Manhattan. But again, he would not stay still, founding two more companies—Tiffany Furnaces and L.C. Tiffany Furnaces.

Although we associate Tiffany with high society, his aim was always very democratic and very American—to "bridge the fine arts and the decorative arts," and to make beauty available to everyone.

Even today, Tiffany sells many inexpensive items that anyone can buy. And there's still something about receiving one of those distinctive blue boxes as a gift that makes you feel like somebody thinks you're very special.

Victor Durand: A Tiffany For New Jersey

New Jersey's contribution to the American glass industry has always been a source of great of pride for the state. After all, Salem County was home to the first commercially successful glass factory in the Western Hemisphere back in the early 1700s, and at one time there were over 100 glass factories operating in the state, most of them in South Jersey.

Before that all came to an end by the middle of the 20th Century, there would be one more flash of glory. This is that story.

Victor Durand, Jr. was born in Baccarat, France, in 1870.

Kids must have grown up faster back then, because in 1884, at the tender age of 14, young Victor had already apprenticed at the famous Baccarat glass factory and was on his way to join his father working at the Whitall-Tatum & Co. glass factory in Millville, New Jersey, USA.

By 1897, the Durands, *père et fils* decided they were ready to strike out on their own. They leased the Vineland Glass Manufacturing Company and created the Vineland Flint Glass Works to make inexpensive scientific glass for pharmaceutical and medical use.

They were so successful that by 1920 they had four different companies working out of the one factory and had expanded their production to include such profitable wholesale items as towel bars, thermos liners and lightbulbs.

Since his days in Baccarat, however, Victor, Jr. had always dreamed of making art glass. In 1924 he got his opportunity, and it came via Brooklyn, New York.

A former associate of Tiffany, Martin Bach, had started a company called Quezal in 1900 to make Tiffany-style iridescent art glass in Brooklyn.

When Bach died in 1924, Durand convinced his son, Martin, Jr. to bring the other Quezal/Tiffany artists—Emil Larsen, William Weidenbine and Harry Britten—to join him in Vineland and create what they would call the "fancy shop" to make Tiffany-style art glass.

With so many glass artists happily at work in the middle of the prosperous "Roaring Twenties," they couldn't help but be a success.

Just two years earlier, in 1922, King Tut's tomb was unearthed and the Durand artists were right there with patterns like King Tut and Egyptian Crackle. Other patterns like Peacock Feather, and Pulled Feather, Venetian Lace, Oriental and Moorish Crackle also fed the demand for stylish Art Deco pieces.

Durand and company further enhanced their reputation in 1926 by winning awards at the Philadelphia Sesquicentennial International Exposition celebrating the 150th anniversary of the signing of the Declaration of Independence.

Only about 30 percent of Durand pieces are signed. When they are, it is with the name "DURAND," hand-written in capital letters with a silver-finish aluminum pencil. Often the name will appear inside a large letter "V." Sometimes numbers are a part of the mark.

Victor Durand died in a car crash in 1931. His company was taken over by Kimble Glass, which operated it for a year and then closed it down.

To learn more about Durand glass, find Edward Meschi's book, "Durand: The Man and His Glass" (The Glass Press, 1998).

Better yet, go down to South Jersey and see all of New Jersey's glass history, including Durand, on exhibit at the fabulous Wheaton Museum of American Glass in Millville.

The Truth About Loetz

There is so much misinformation about Loetz glass, even in the most reputable antiques books. Let's set the story straight.

Johann Loetz did not found the company that bears his name. He probably never worked for or with Louis Comfort Tiffany. And there was no such person as Johann Loetz Witwe. Here's the real story.

We know very little about Johann Loetz (1778-1844). It is quite possible that he worked in the Austrian/Bohemian glass industry, and it may even be likely, as legend has it, that he was among the earliest to experiment with the kind of iridescent art glass that eventually made Tiffany famous. It may even be possible that Tiffany was aware of and maybe even studied Loetz's experiments. These "facts," however, are only speculation and hearsay, perhaps perpetrated as company publicity.

What we do know is that after Loetz's death his wife, Susanna, remarried. In 1851, she and her new husband, Dr. Franz Gerstner bought a glass factory in the Bohemian town of Kastersky Mlyn, better known by its German name, Klostermühle.

They named the glass works "Johan Loetz Witwe," meaning Johann Loetz's widow. Apparently, Johann Loetz was very well known among the glass artists of the area, and they used his name to add prestige to the new company.

Loetz may also have left his widow the glass formulas with which they started the business. That way the factory and formulas could finance the education of their grandson, Maximillian Ritter Von Spaun II, with a legacy from his grandfather.

In any event, the glass factory did finance Max's education, and in 1879, after he had graduated with a degree in engineering, Susanna turned the business entirely over to him.

Max completely overhauled the business, turning production away from utilitarian household glassware to luxury art glass. He hired the best managers and glass artists he could find, and within a decade the company was exhibiting at the finest glass and decorative art exhibitions in Europe, including the famous Paris Exhibition of 1900, where it won a gold and two silver medals.

The big winner at that fair was Louis Comfort Tiffany. So, the Loetz company decided to market, "affordable art glass in the Tiffany style." This strategy was quite effective, resulting in Loetz glass decorating more homes than Tiffany. Even those who could afford Tiffany also featured affordable Loetz.

The company fell out of family hands in the 1930s, and went out of business in 1947. Aside from some distinctively Art Deco pieces from the 1920s, Loetz glass from the period 1880 to the 1920s is what is the most sought after today.

Green was the most popular color at the turn of the century, and the Loetz company, always willing to accommodate public taste, produced a great deal of wares in that color. Most collectors will already have some neat pieces in green, so they will be looking for other colors, like gold, amethyst, ruby and the marble glass line called "*Marmorierte Glas*" (1880-1910). Therefore, non-green pieces may cost a bit more because of that demand.

Very little Loetz glass is signed, so it's helpful to familiarize yourself with it when you find it identified in reputable shops. Most Loetz glass will have a recessed, polished pontil mark. However, some top-blown pieces will have flat bottoms that seem to swirl in the middle—a result of being turned by the glassblower.

Some Tiffany-style iridescent Loetz glass will bear a bogus Tiffany signature. This was not done by the company, but by unscrupulous dealers of the time. Oddly enough, these bogus marked Tiffany pieces will command a bit of a premium over regular Loetz prices.

Loetz is still the "affordable Tiffany," with prices in the average range of $300 to $1,000. At about 20 percent of what a similar Tiffany would be, Loetz is a real bargain, and since Loetz was more commonly found than Tiffany in the homes of the period, this beautiful art glass is a wonderful way to achieve an authentic turn-of-the-century look.

The Art Glass Of Bohemia

◆

From Moser to Czecho-Deco

In every European language, the term "bohemian" is used to describe any free-spirited artist. The real Bohemians, however, have rarely been free, at least not politically. The Kingdom of Bohemia in eastern Europe has been a conquered nation for most of its history, dominated at various times by the Romans, the Turks, the Austrians, Nazi Germany and Communist Russia.

The royal family of Bohemia was the Premslid dynasty, founded on an ancient legend about the poor plowboy, Premsyl, who caught the eye of the wealthy young princess, Lubisa. The Premslids found it much more fun to fight among themselves than rule a kingdom and the Bohemian people, mostly nomadic clans, were happy to let them.

After all, kings are just plowboys who got lucky. In fact, no matter who conquered or ruled them, the Bohemians have always been a free-spirited people, a characteristic that probably helped them become among the finest artists in Europe.

Artists, however, need more than self-confidence and a free spirit. They need to know their craft, and the Bohemians learned well, especially from the Romans. It was the Romans who taught the Bohemians to make fine ceramics, and the skill for which they would become world-renown—glassmaking.

The Bohemians excelled at every aspect of glass making: coloring, shaping, cutting and decorating. And like true artists, they were not just skillful technicians, but also imaginative, creative and inventive.

Among the most artistic of the Bohemian glassmakers was Ludwig Moser (1833-1916). Moser started out by making fanciful souvenir wares to be sold to the wealthy visitors at the posh health spas of Austria.

In 1857 Moser opened the first of what would eventually be three glassmaking studios in Karlsbad, Bohemia. For the next 41 years, until his death in 1916, Moser made some of the finest art glass and elegant tableware in the world. It was collected throughout Europe and was a particular favorite of well-to-do Victorians in both England and the United States.

Moser created glass with deeply etched and complex engravings, but he is probably best known for refining two standard Bohemian techniques: cut overlay and applied enamel.

In cut overlay, also called "cut-to-clear," a layer of colored glass is coated over clear glass. A design is then hand-cut into the colored glass to reveal the clear glass underneath. Bohemians were famous for this type of glass, especially for the rich, gem-quality colors of ruby, emerald green, cobalt and cranberry. Grapes and vines were a favorite design, and were imitated around the world. Hunt scenes, featuring deer and castles, were also popular.

Moser's most stunning achievement, however, was in gilt and enamel work. For these pieces he chose colors like the world has never seen before or since—a subtle green, wispy amber, pale blue or a light cranberry—sometimes fading them very gradually to crystal clear. The pieces were then decorated with heavy gold and painted with enamels, like icing on a cake, in complex arabesques or continuously scrolling vines, punctuated with delicate leaves.

Moser's pieces are rarely signed, but to a collector, the artistry is signature enough. Some powerfully spectacular art glass has created over the years, but none, absolutely none, as charming, as elegant or as superbly artistic as Moser's.

After World War I, the Kingdom of Bohemia became a part of the new Republic of Czecho-slovakia (the hyphen disappeared sometime in the 1920s). Moser's sons continued the business until 1922, when the firm merged with another Bohemian company, Meyr's Neffe.

By the mid-1920s, Czech glassmakers continued the Bohemian art glass tradition by dominating the Art Deco movement with sleek, streamlined, futuristic design as well as creating affordable copies of such Deco glass artists as Rene Lalique. So important are Czechoslovakian accessories to Art Deco design, that collectors now refer to them as "Czecho-Deco."

In 1939, Hitler invaded Czechoslovakia, and after World War II, the country fell behind the Iron Curtain. As of January 1, 1994, the country ceased to exist, breaking up into Slovakia and the Czech Republic, which now includes Bohemia. Pieces marked "Czechoslovakia" now have a definite time frame (1918-1993), so expect their value to rise as time goes by.

Good Scents Collecting

"All the perfumes of Arabia ..." says Lady Macbeth, and looney as the lady is, she makes good sense about scents.

Although we associate perfumes with the French, they actually originated in the Middle East. Two of the three gifts of the Magi—myrrh and frankincense—were perfumes, and they were very valuable offerings, certainly equal to the third gift of gold.

The word "perfume" is of Latin origin, however, meaning "through smoke." It refers to the Roman practice of scenting fires with certain concoctions to produce pleasing aromas in the homes of the wealthy during special occasions or for religious ceremonies.

The earliest examples we have of perfume containers are Egyptian. These containers are made of such materials as alabaster, onyx and terra cotta. But the Egyptians were also the first masters of art glass, and records indicate they produced art glass perfume bottles as early as 1500 B.C. in colors that imitated natural gems and hard stones.

Art glass perfume bottles are still favored by today's collectors, especially those produced during the art glass explosion of the Victorian era, those from the turn-of-the-century Art Nouveau period, and the Art Deco designs of the 1920s and '30s.

From what we know of the bathing habits of the Victorians, and the stench of the big cities of that era, there was certainly reason to load up on pleasant scents if you could afford them.

Victorians bought their scents from the drugstore in large, nondescript commercial bottles, and brought them back home to be decanted in a wide variety of fancy art glass bottles.

Among the finest early Victorian-era perfume bottles are those created from the 1830s on by the Stourbridge firms of Stevens and Williams and Thomas Webb, as well as the decorated opal ware of the various firms operating in the city of Bristol.

Also prized among Victorian perfume bottle collectors are French Baccarat crystal (beginning in 1845), Bohemian overlay, gilt and enameled glass, American Mt. Washington glass and colorful French "opaline" glass.

American "Brilliant Cut" glass, a heavy crystal with deep and complex cuts, took the world by storm when it was introduced at the Philadelphia Centennial Exhibition in 1876. Perfume bottles in this style are hard to find in good condition.

The turn-of-the-century Art Nouveau movement saw the entrance of great glass artists like Tiffany, Daum and Galle into the perfume bottle business. Also from this period, look for silver overlay perfume bottles.

Some perfume collectors are only interested in commercial perfume bottles, which started appearing at the end of the 19th Century. Now there would be no need to decant your perfume; the bottle it came in was a work of art in itself.

The trend began with the French firm Guerlain, but the big step in commercial bottles came in 1907 when Francois Coty asked French jewelry designer, René Lalique, to design a label for his perfume. Instead, Lalique designed the bottle, and the rest is history.

Lalique commercial perfume bottles, from 1910 through the 1950s, are among the most sought-after by collectors.

One of the biggest advances in perfumes at the turn of the century was the atomizer, and what an interesting story it is.

An American medical doctor, Allen DeVilbis, who specialized in nose and throat ailments, initially developed the atomizer to help his patients.

Much to his father's dismay, his son, Thomas, saw the potential in these atomizers for delivering perfume. His father opposed such a frivolous application of his medical patent, but finally relented, and in July of 1910 Thomas was granted a patent for a perfume atomizer.

Perfumers with a "DeVilbis" mark on the atomizer can cost around $300 or more, depending on who made the glass. Steuben glass is one of the most desirable.

Also among the most favored Art Deco perfume bottles are those from Czechoslovakia. Czech crystal perfume bottles are recognizable by their tall and flashy stoppers in classic Art Deco designs.

Don't forget to look for other good scents collectibles, including: potpourri jars and containers, lilac and rose water jars, salts jars (for smelling salts), vinaigrettes, fancy old incense burners and scent sconces.

Pressed Pattern Glass

From the Civil War of the 1860s up through the 1920s, pattern glass dinnerware was an important part of everyday life in most middle-class and upper-middle-class American homes. Some families even had more than one set. But the story of pattern glass actually began about 40 years earlier.

In 1820, Demming Jarvis received a patent for a process called "pressed glass," where molten glass was actually pressed into a mold that formed a shape and left a design in relief. By 1828 his process was in full use at the Boston and Sandwich Glass Company in Sandwich, Massachusetts.

Jarvis's patent was just the first of many, and before long most glass companies were equipped with some sort of glass-pressing machinery. While molded glass had been made before, even back in ancient times, it could now be mass-produced on a large scale.

Traditional glassblowing was very labor intensive, requiring skilled craftsmen. The pressed-glass machines, however, could be operated by laborers and they produced more glass. As a result, more American-made glass products became available and affordable to more Americans.

By the 1860s many glass factories had all the different machinery in place to produce full and extensive dinnerware services. Most pattern glass pieces were produced by the pressed-glass process, but some were mold-blown, that is, blown into a molded pattern.

You can tell the mold-blown pieces by the pontil mark, the scar on the bottom left by the blower's rod. It was the pressed-glass process, however, that made the production of so many extensive sets of dishes possible.

There were literally hundreds of different patterns of glass dinnerware produced during the 60 years of pattern-glass popularity. Many of these were based on European and American cut-glass geometric designs including diamonds, pinwheels, stars, circles and bulls'eyes.

By the 1880s and '90s, however, glass companies used improved technology to become bolder and more inventive.

They created patterns with figural finials, stems and pedestals. They used more color and colorful stains, and produced more frosted (acid-washed) detail. Some designs had stippled backgrounds, a close, intricate pattern of dots that resembles frosting.

So, with all that going for them, why are most pattern-glass pieces still so inexpensive? The reason is that most people, including dealers, still think of them as cheap glass, and there is a widespread fear of reproduction.

Most patterns can be easily identified with a bit of research, and we can usually pinpoint the company name, city and date of manufacture.

The process for identifying unfamiliar patterns is first to check "The Collectors Encyclopedia of Pattern Glass" by Mollie Helen McCain (Collector Books), where patterns are sorted by shape and drawn in detail. Some patterns are so intricately detailed they don't show well in photos.

Manufacturing information and prices on many collectible table settings are available in Jenks and Luna's "Early American Pattern Glass (1850-1910)" (Wallace Homestead). This book also includes a reproduction alert.

Reproduction pattern glass tends to be thicker and heavier than it should be. The glass itself may be of poor quality, off color, crinkled, or too slick. Reproduced patterns are never exactly like the originals. Either they are too exaggeratedly detailed or have hardly any detail.

Putting together a complete table service in one pattern is a noble enterprise, but it's nearly impossible to do by just going antiquing. You have to get involved in the collector clubs and do some heavy networking.

Most folks like to collect a particular shape—celery vase, spooner vase, banana compote (folded up at the sides), square cake plates, pitchers, goblets, cordials and tumblers. You can put together a varied collection of these that are fun to use and display.

By the way, if you want your pattern glass to sparkle like crystal, clean it with some scratch-less cleanser (Bon Ami), a soft toothbrush and lukewarm water.

Opal, Opaline, Opalescent

Opal, opaline, opalescent. Does it sound like I'm conjugating a highly irregular old Greek verb? Well, if these words are Greek to you, you're missing out on some of the most popularly collectible decorative art glass on today's antiques market.

Opalizing glass, that is, giving it a milky quality, is a centuries-old glassmaking technique. It involves adding calcium phosphate (bone ash) to the glass and firing the piece twice. Glassmakers as far back as the 1600s called items made in this fashion, "Opal Ware," and it was most often hand-painted and marketed at a low cost to compete with high-priced porcelains.

This opal glass was densely opaque (not translucent), and today it is listed in the antique guides by its common nickname, "Milk Glass." The earliest milk glass we are likely to find on today's market is late 19th Century Victorian vintage. The milk glass we usually see in any quantity was probably made in the 1930s through the 1950s by Fenton Glass or Westmoreland.

How can you tell the old from the new? The newer glass tends to be a starker white, shinier and slicker to the touch. At fifty years old or more, however, some Fenton patterns are gaining their own fans and gaining in value, as are some Westmoreland items from as recent as the 1970s.

When glass is washed with acid, its sheen is dulled to a frosted finish called "satin glass." Satin milk glass was popular in Victorian times, especially in lamps and personal items, like humidors, jewelry boxes and vanity pieces. One of the finest American producers of this type of glass was the Mt. Washington Company of Boston and New Bedford, Massachusetts.

Much of Mt. Washington's satin milk glass was sent for decorating to the studios of C.F. Monroe in Meriden, Connecticut. Many of these elaborately painted pieces were marketed by Monroe from 1892 to 1916 under the trade name, "Wave Crest," for the foamy white caps of the sea.

In the city of Bristol, England, back in the early 1700s, glassmakers produced a kind of semi-opaque milk glass known as "opaline." It, too, was hand-painted and, like opal ware and Wave Crest, was created to compete with porcelain. This style glass became quite popular, especially in lamps, boxes and vases, and was soon produced in Germany, France and the United States. Wherever it is produced, these wares are called "Bristol Glass," and we are more likely to find late Victorian pieces from the 1880s and '90s on today's antiques market.

The term "opaline" is usually reserved for truly translucent pieces—usually in colors like blue, green and pink—that have a barely milky quality throughout the color that gives the piece a soft glow in the light. Although it was produced around the world, from Britain to Bohemia, some of the finest opaline, especially in blue, was created in France around the turn of the century.

In Vineland, New Jersey, in the 1930s, they produced a curious style of opaline. Kimball Glass (the company that bought Durand Glass after Victor Durand died in a car crash in 1931) created a blotchy opaline called "cluthra," a word meaning "clouds." Steuben Glass of Corning, New York, also made a cluthra line.

Without a doubt, the type of opal glass that's driving collectors craziest today is the type known as "Opalescent Glass." This is what we call glass that is trimmed or decorated with opal. Collectors are particularly interested in the colorful pieces produced during the pre-World War I Edwardian era from 1890 to 1915.

Opalescent glass can be blown (usually mold-blown) or pressed. Blown items were especially difficult to make, and are characterized by opal decoration throughout the piece in designs like dots, swirls, lace and lattice.

Pressed-glass opalescent pieces were produced by the major pattern-glass companies like Dugan, Northwood and the companies of the U.S. Glass conglomerate. These are characterized by opal trimmings around the rims or highlighting some of the raised design of the mold.

How To Speak Italian Glass

The tradition of glassmaking in Italy has its roots in ancient times. Through the Roman Empire, the Italians learned glassmaking techniques from the Phoenicians (today's Syrians), who, according to legend, invented glass, and the Egyptians, who turned glass into the stuff of art by fashioning it into jewelry and exquisite decorative objects.

By the Renaissance (15th and 16th Centuries), the tiny island of Murano off the coast of Venice had become the dominant glassmaking center in the world. In fact, the techniques employed by the artists of Murano were considered as important as state secrets, and were so highly guarded that the glassmakers were kept virtual prisoners on their island.

This all changed with the passage of time, and Murano eventually had to share the market with the rest of the world—Bohemia, Scandinavia, Germany, England, France and, by the 19th Century, the United States.

During the first decade of the Modern Movement in the 1920s, however, Murano started its ascent to the top of the glassmaking world once more. Largely through the efforts of Italian glass artist Paolo Venini, Murano would again become a dominant art glass center, this time for twenty years, from 1945 to 1965.

Venini saw that the old Murano techniques were particularly suited to the fluid, organic Modern Movement designs. His work fueled another Murano Renaissance and a revival of some of those once jealously guarded glassmaking techniques.

Many of these Murano techniques involved the use of colorful glass rods called canes. In one technique, several of these different colored canes were heated and stretched as long and as thinly as possible. Then the thin canes were bunched together, reheated and sliced.

As you might imagine, when you look down at one of these slices of bunched together canes, what you see resembles a flower. Put many of these flowers together, some even from different bunches of canes, and what you get is a technique called "millefiori," common in glass paperweights.

"Millefiori" in Italian means a thousand flowers. To understand and talk about Italian glass, it helps to learn how to speak the language of Italian glass. It's fun—millefiore, murrina, aventurina, bullicante, filigrano, sommerso, latticino—and when it doesn't sound romantic, it sounds like something good is cooking in the kitchen.

Two of these techniques also involving glass canes are: filigrano, where thin filigrees or filaments of glass are striped or swirled within a piece of glass; and latticino, where those filaments crisscross to form a lattice.

The technique where stripes of colored glass are set within a piece of glass is known by the nickname, "ribbon glass." Including patches of colored glass canes results in "murrina," after an ornamental stone the Romans sometimes embedded in their pottery.

"Bullicante," literally "bubbling," is the Italian word for bubble glass. In a process called "inclusion," bubbles are included into a piece of glass using a special glassblowing attachment called a crimp. This crimp consists of a series of little nozzles that each deposit a bubble of air into the glass when the glassmaker blows through it. Different crimps can produce regular or scattered patterns.

Bullicante glass is often used in paperweights, and as a heavy base for bowls, vases and figurines. In a special technique, called "reticello," bubbles are artfully included inside the diamond-shaped crisscrosses of a latticino.

Cased glass, where a layer of glass is sandwiched between two others, is a common glass technique, especially among the Bohemians or the Czechs. In Italian glass, however, when thick layers of glass can be seen inside each other, it is called by what it looks like—"sommerso," or submerged glass.

The Murano glass artists are also well known for including metal into glass. Thin sheets of copper or gold leaf may be included whole or in pieces, or blown asunder by the glassblower into glittering metallic specks. This technique is called "aventurina." I don't know what the word means literally, but it sounds as impressive as the glass looks.

The shapes of many Venetian glass objects, especially the bowls, plates and trays, were perfect Modern Movement designs—asymmetrical, elliptical and often globular, rather than geometric. These shapes are called "organic" or "biomorphic," meaning life shapes, because they resemble stylized versions of living things—amoeba, protozoa, heart, kidney, flower, leaf, clover. Some shapes, called "geodes," look like chunks of rock mined right from the earth.

The Murano artists also produced an array of sculptured glass figurines—people, animals, birds and fish.

A less colorful and more subdued "smoke" glass, a transparent black glass, was extremely popular from around 1958 to1962.

Signed pieces of Italian glass are rare and highly prized, especially those by Venini, who died in 1959. Most companies used paper labels, and collectors prefer they remain intact. Other companies to look for include: Seguso, Salviati, Barbini, Barovier and Toso.

Some companies are distinguished by the distinctive techniques they employed the most. The best way recognize them is to become familiar with these techniques, and to learn more about speaking the language of Italian glass.

New Prosperity For Depression Glass

Much of Depression glass's charm, as with so many antiques, is in its story. Far from being depressing, this was the uplifting glass that added color and a touch of grace to the lives of people who were struggling through that devastating economic hardship called The Great Depression (1929-1939).

The marketing of American-made glass dinnerware also helped to stimulate sales and create jobs during those difficult times. Free pieces could be had simply by going to a movie, getting a tank of gas, buying a box of soap or saving grocery store receipts. Folks would swap patterns or fill out their sets by buying more pieces at a hardware store or at the "five-and-dime."

Because of the very nature of its mass production, Depression glass is an inferior glass. Molds were overused, so patterns are sometimes muddy or uneven. Fuel conservation resulted in fires that often didn't get hot enough to allow batches of glass to release their gases, which caused bubble inclusions in the finished pieces.

These occasional imperfections never deterred collectors, however. Depression glass was otherwise colorful, plentiful, still useful and, for the most part, affordable. The glitches were just part of its charm.

Although there may be as many as a couple of hundred patterns of Depression glass, collectors have traditionally gone for those with fancy, fine-line patterns that resemble etched glass—Princess, American Sweetheart, Cameo (Dancing Girl), Madrid, Cherry Blossom, Sharon (Cabbage Rose), Mayfair, Cupid, Florentine, and others. The preferred color was always pink, with green a close second.

These patterns still top collectors' lists, but as tastes change, and experts find and identify additional patterns that were not listed before, a whole different array of patterns and colors have been rising in poularity.

Patterns in the Art Deco style of the 1930s, for instance, have never been as popular as they are now. These are patterns that emphasize shape rather than decoration, and their designs are more geometric and modern looking.

Patterns like Pyramid, Manhattan, Tea Room, Moderntone, Moondrops, Ring (Banded Rings), Mt. Pleasant (Double Shield) and New Century, just to name a few, are extremely high-style designs.

Aside from the traditional pink and green, collectors are now looking for unusual colors, even in traditional designs. Mayfair, for instance was also produced in frost and frosted pink; American Sweetheart, in cobalt and in the unusual "monax" color (a translucent, iridescent white, sometimes trimmed with pink) and in red, blue, yellow, and a dark gray called "smoke."

There has also been increasing interest in opaque or semi-opaque Depression glass, a type long avoided by collectors. Vitrock, for instance, was a milk glass line produced by Hocking from 1934 to 1937. Also called Flower Rim, because of its embossed floral border, it can be plain white or decorated with a blue decal of a classical scene, called the Lake Como pattern.

Indiana Custard, also called Flower and Leaf Band because of its embossed border, was produced by the Indiana Glass Co. throughout the 1930s and again in the 1950s. It is an off-white color, which the company called French Ivory, and it may have floral decal decoration.

The L. E. Smith Company produced many black glass patterns that have a stylish Art Deco look. Also in the Art Deco style is the Ovide pattern by Hazel Atlas, a translucent white with red or red and black horizontal striping.

It's useless to give representative prices for Depression glass, because prices vary so widely between patterns and even within patterns. A relatively inexpensive pattern, for instance, may have a few pieces that are very rare and therefore quite pricey.

Unfortunately, several Depression glass patterns were heavily reproduced during the 1970s and '80s. Collectors have to be more sophisticated these days, especially when buying off the Internet.

Sometimes we forget we are now in the 21st Century, and that in less than 30 years Depression glass pieces will be over 100 years old and full-fledged antiques.

What wonderful antiques they will be, too. Talk about evoking the times in which they were made! Bright colors, cheery patterns, forward-looking designs, all working to spur on business during the darkest economic times this country has ever known, Depression glass is a tribute to that special spark that made the 1900s the American Century.

The Multiple Personalities Of Steuben Glass

Steuben, the company that by sheer longevity and consistency of quality became the premier American art glass house of the 20th Century, was started by two Englishmen.

Thomas Hawkes and Frederick Carder opened the Steuben Glass Works in Corning, New York in 1903. The company was named for Steuben County, where the city of Corning is located.

Frederick Carder (1863-1963) was brought to this country by his fellow countryman, Thomas Hawkes, who was already in business cutting, etching and decorating glass blanks made for him by the Corning Glass Works. The idea was for Hawkes to provide the financing and for Carder to run the company, providing blank glass for Hawkes to decorate. Carder, however, was too restless an artist ever to be content just to make glass for some other person to decorate.

An incredible artistic and technical genius in his own right, he had been a glassmaker since the age of 13, and by age 18 he was designing and creating art glass for Stevens and Williams, one of England's finest glass houses. He won medals in several national competitions, and by the age of 28 he had set up his own school to instruct talented glass workers in design and techniques. So it was no surprise to anyone, when in 1904, only one year after the founding of Steuben, Carder patented a glass technique that would make him famous, be widely imitated, and establish Steuben as a leading force in American art glass.

Carder called the technique "Aurene." The name came from combining the Latin word *aurum*, for gold, with *schene*, a Middle English spelling of "sheen" or "shine."

The process called for gold or blue colored glass to be sprayed "at the fire" with a solution of tin and/or iron chloride. This produced a rich, velvety, iridescent luster on the surface of the glass and—on some of the larger pieces—a series of thin radiating lines throughout the piece.

Aurene brought iridescent glass, made popular by Tiffany, to new heights. But more important is what the Aurene process did to the colors of the glass. The gold is an incredibly deep gold, sometimes with red or purple shadings. The blues come out in a variety of shadings, from silver and gold to rich red-violet to some greenish tones.

Next Carder produced a line called "Verre de Soie" (silk glass) with an iridescent silken shine that played a rainbow of colors in the light. Tyrian glass, invented in 1916, was named for the ancient city of Tyre, where the Phoenicians developed a purple dye from mollusk shells, and made purple the color of royalty ever since.

Steuben Tyrian pieces aren't just purple, however. Some come off as a bluish green and others a deep blue, both with a purplish blush. Often pieces were further decorated with glass threading or details in applied Aurene glass.

In 1918, Steuben became the Steuben Division of the Corning Glass Works, but Carder was still the boss and continued to patent an array of colorful art glass in groundbreaking techniques.

Carder's artistic colors included: Alabaster (iridescent opaline), Cluthra (cloudy white), and the gem-like Rose Quartz, Amethyst Quartz and Celeste.

He also created porcelain-like glass in Ivory, Mandarin Yellow, and Rouge Flambé, hard stone colors like Plum Jade and Diatria (reddish marble), and an impossibly thin cased glass called Intarsia.

Carder left Steuben in 1932, but it is the glass from his tenure there (1903-1932) that most excites collectors today.

After he left, Steuben would never make colorful art glass again. Instead, the company began production of the clear liquid crystal it is known for to this day.

The change in Steuben began with Arthur A. Houghton Jr., who would rule the company from 1933 to 1973. In contrast to Carder, the temperamental, hands-on, creative artist, Houghton was an even-tempered aristocrat, a connoisseur, a keen businessman and a brilliant organizer. It is amazing how the glass Steuben produced under each of these men so perfectly reflects their different personalities.

Collectors have already begun to show interest in the pure form, crystal sculptures of later Steuben, especially those designed by some of the fine artists Houghton managed to assemble.

Look for such names as George Thompson, Walter Heintze, Paul Schulze, John Dreves, Pavel Tchelitchew, Lloyd Atkins and Donald Pollard.

Much of Steuben glass is not signed or marked on the glass. Various paper labels were used over the years and have been lost with time. The most common early Steuben mark, aside from pieces just signed by Carder, was the acid stamped fleur-de-lis behind a banner with Steuben in block letters.

About 1929, the name Steuben was often etched in block letters or script. After 1932, the company either used that mark or just a simple "S." The current most common mark is the company name inside an oval. As usual, marked or signed pieces will command the premium.

PART V
Stories About Metals
And Jewelry

Sterling Remembrances * Coin Silver—Uniquely American * The Jolly
Rogers * Moonlight In Denmark * The Mexican *Plateros* * Copper's
Not Just Pennies Anymore * Mining For Old Aluminum * Cameos,
The Heirloom Jewelry * The Magic of Gemstones * It's Tole For Thee
* Never Go Walking Out Without Your Hatpin * Chasing After Chase
* The Man Who Wouldn't Give Waltham The Time * Fabulous Fakes
With Real Names * Beauty Was Their Business

Sterling Remembrances

I've always been fond of silver. Sure, gold is brilliantly beautiful and aggressively rich. But it's also at least ten times more costly than silver.

Silver is called the "moon metal," and has a softer glow—moody and romantic. Although silver may be more subtle than gold, a dining table laden with silver flatware, serving pieces and candelabra is still quite breathtaking. A well-lit cabinet crammed with a gleaming collection of silver can be an impressive sight indeed.

The first thing we should remember about sterling silver is how it got its name. It's quite an interesting story.

In the year 1300, King John of England needed a silver coin that couldn't be broken. Silver is a very soft metal, and pure silver coins easily could be broken into parts—which is exactly what John's subjects were doing to pay for things.

So the king wanted a coin that had the highest amount of silver possible while still being strong enough to stay a whole coin. Eventually he found a group of German metal craftsmen living in England, who had a reputation for creating a formula for producing sturdy items with a very high silver content—92.5 percent.

Because their homeland in Germany was east of England, these Germans were called "Easterlings," and King John ordered all silver made in England to be "of Easterling allayed" (he meant alloyed), and to be marked "Easterling Silver." Over the years, the first two letters were dropped, and in 1596, sterling silver (.925 silver) became the standard for all English silver items.

In the rebellious American colonies, however, the standard was .900 silver, also called "Coin Silver" or "American Standard." In 1840, America adopted the sterling standard.

Remembering all that, silver has long been a way of remembering all sorts of things.

For instance, the idea of collecting spoons as remembrances goes back 500 years to the Renaissance in Europe, when it became the custom to collect "apostle spoons." These were spoons with handles crafted in the full figure shape of each of Christ's twelve apostles.

Up until that time, only the Church or wealthy aristocrats could afford to own precious metals. Apostle spoons gave folks of moderate means the opportunity and the incentive to invest in silver by purchasing each spoon as they could afford it.

To start you on your way, your first apostle spoon would be a gift from your godparents at your baptism. Thus we have the expression, "to be born with a silver spoon in your mouth."

Today some folks still give sterling baby spoons to newborns. But in, 1881, a man named Myron Kinsley thought that newlyweds, prospective parents to be, might be interested in starting their investment early.

Kinsley came up with the idea for a sterling souvenir spoon for Niagara Falls, which had already become a honeymoon capital. His spoon featured the full figure of an American Indian, and it was such a big hit that other tourist destinations began to issue sterling souvenir spoons of their own.

The spoon that started the craze for collecting sterling souvenirs, however, was created in 1890 for Salem, Massachusetts by Daniel Lowe. It featured a handle crafted as an evil-eyed witch with her broomstick. The next year, 1891, he added a crescent moon and an arched-back black cat to the handle.

By that year, the craze for collecting souvenir spoons had become nothing short of a phenomenon. Only 18 months after Lowe's first Salem spoon, there were over 2, 200 different souvenir spoon designs in circulation in the United States.

The height of souvenir spoon production occurred between 1890 to 1914. World War I saw production decline, but it quickly revived in the Roaring 1920s. The advent of the automobile had more people traveling, with some folks taking trips to places just to collect the spoons.

Not only towns and cities issued special spoons, however. Sterling and silver plate souvenir spoons were crafted for colleges and universities, famous buildings and monuments, world's fairs and exhibitions, special events, anniversaries, coronations, and even as advertising premiums.

Just about every antique shop has some souvenir spoons, and their availability and affordability are making them collector favorites today. They are also very portable and easy to display. And because they are usually demitasse spoons or teaspoons, they make interesting conversation pieces at dessert time.

More importantly, souvenir spoons are among the finest examples of late 19th and early 20th Century silver craftsmanship. Look especially for full figures and pieces that have details on the reverse as well as the front.

Detail is the name of the game in souvenir spoons, whether they are silver plate or sterling. The more elaborate the details—the fur of an animal, the texture of clothing, bricks in the building, designs in the bowl as well as on the handle—the more attractive the spoon will be to a collector.

Most collectors will collect any spoon that catches their fancy. Others will specialize—only Indians, military themes, schools or world's fairs, for instance. As with postcards, souvenir spoons tend to be more valuable in the places they come from.

Coin Silver—Uniquely American

With both silver and Americana topping collectors' lists, it stands to reason that the perfect crossover collectible would be old coin silver, a uniquely American silver concoction.

In colonial America, silver objects were hard to come by. There were no silver mines, and only the wealthy could afford to have sterling imported from England. One alternative was to bring silver coins to a local smithy to have him melt them down and fashion them into objects. Thus the term, "coin silver."

The metalsmiths added extra metal to the silver to make them strong enough to serve as utensils and serving pieces. Their formula was 900/1000 parts silver, and that would become the American standard for silver from the 1600s until about 1840.

From the 1840s on, more and more American silversmiths began making sterling silver, and eventually sterling would officially become the American standard in 1860.

Most early American coin silver is not marked as such. The term "coin silver" might have been in common use for many years before 1820, but it doesn't appear on pieces until around that date.

An identifying mark you might see on pieces made before or after 1820 is "Standard," but more than likely the piece will just be stamped with a maker's mark.

To determine if the maker who marked your piece specialized in coin silver, you will need to do some research.

Three good reference guides are: the "Encyclopedia of American Silver Manufacturers" by Dorothy Rainwater (Schiffer), "The Book of Old Silver" by Seymour Wyler (Crown), and "Kovel's American Silver Marks" (Crown).

When you find a maker you will find the years that he worked. Of course, pieces by those few 17th Century makers will be more valuable. But most of the items you will find on today's market are from the mid-18th to early 19th Centuries.

You can also spot coin silver by its appearance. Since silversmiths tried to make the most of the silver they had to work with, most coin silver pieces are fashioned very thinly and in simple shapes.

Monograms actually enhance the value of coin silver items. Silver makers were very proud of their engraving skill and loved to show it off.

You may find decoration on the backs of utensils made of coin silver; this is because tables were set with utensils facing down. This even holds true for serving spoons.

Spoons are the most common items found in coin silver, because they were the most needed. Up until about 1860, most Americans used only spoons for dining, and sometimes knives, if something needed cutting. Most folks used their fingers to eat. Forks were common only in the wealthiest of households and for special occasions.

Coin silver is a wonderful part of American history, unique to us. Polished pieces display beautifully in a cabinet and are fun to use, especially for particularly American feasts like Thanksgiving.

The Jolly Rogers

There's a piece of Rogers silver plate somewhere in your home. Maybe it's that tea set or set of flatware you inherited.

Even if it's not that obvious, check around—in that junk drawer in the kitchen, or in the drawer under the dining room china cabinet. Just about everybody in America has something with the Rogers name on it.

That remarkable statement is true mostly because of three talented brothers, William, Simeon and Asa Rogers. Beginning in the early 19th Century, they dominated the silver business in Connecticut, a state that would become a hotbed for America's industrial revolution and give rise to the expression "Yankee ingenuity."

It all started in 1820, when William Rogers, the eldest of the brothers, left the family farm to become an apprentice to Joseph Church, a jeweler and silversmith in Hartford, Connecticut. In just five years, he became Church's partner. They made coin silver (.900 pure, the American standard until 1840) spoons marked Church and Rogers, but William also used his own stamp: "(eagle) Wm. Rogers (star)" from 1825 to 1841.

William brought his two brothers into the firm, and from that time on the three brothers would branch out into the various partnerships, mergers, buyouts and individual enterprises that would make Rogers the most respected name in American silver manufacturing.

In 1836, William Rogers, while still in partnership with Church in Hartford and with his brother Asa in New Britain, became one of the first American silversmiths to produce and market sterling silver (.925 pure) flatware instead of the American standard, coin silver.

It's ironic that one of the first to produce American sterling was a Rogers, because that name would eventually become synonymous with fine American silver plate. That history begins in Granby, CT with Asa Rogers, who began experimenting with electroplating silver in 1843.

The process of electroplating silver had been developed in Birmingham, England in 1836 by George Richards Elkington. Through a series of patents, Elkington had pretty well perfected the process by the early 1840s, when Asa began experimenting.

In 1847, Asa went into partnership with his other two brothers and began producing electroplated silver in Hartford. This is the first time the "Rogers Brothers" stamp was used. They became so successful that, in 1853, they had to start another company—Rogers Bros. Mfg. Co.—to handle the increased volume.

Rogers is a common name, so every silversmith named Rogers in the country tried to cash in on the burgeoning reputation of the original brothers. This led to a proliferation of Rogers stamps on silverplate and some of the confusion in the industry.

C. Rogers & Bros. are three other brothers, who opened shop in 1866 in Meriden, Connecticut. They also started the Rogers Silver Plate Co. in Danbury in 1896. William A. Rogers was a New York silversmith, who began making silver plate in 1894. And there were many more.

By the turn of the century, the large conglomerates, International Silver and Oneida, began buying up the smaller companies. They continued to use the Rogers stamps for the companies belonging to the original three brothers, but not for the others.

You may see a stamp reading: "1847 Rogers Brothers" or "1881 Rogers Brothers." These dates have nothing to do with the age of the piece; they are simply lines of quality silver plate flatware produced by the company,

The best way to date Rogers or any silver plate is by the pattern name, which rarely appears on the piece, but can be found by research in such a book as Tere Hagan's "Silverplate Flatware Identification and Value Guide" (Collector Books, 4th edition, 1995).

Hagan includes line drawings of the handles of hundreds of patterns from about the 1850s through the 1950s, and divides the patterns into sections by company.

The date when the pattern was introduced is also included, and you can assume in most cases that the piece you have was produced not long after that. This is because most companies were always producing new patterns to appeal to the taste and style of the day.

Prices for old silver plate are still very low. Dealers, if they are interested at all, may pay less that 50 cents to a dollar for place-setting pieces, and less than that to nothing at all for monograms (pieces with initials).

There has been quite an active market, however, for pieces from the 1880s to the 1920s in the elaborate patterns of the Victorian, Aesthetic Movement and Art Nouveau styles.

Of particular interest are the serving pieces, especially the unusual ones like cream sauce and punch ladles; mustard, jelly and marmalade spoons; pickle, endive and lettuce forks; tomato servers; ice, sugar and bonbon tongs, and ice spoons.

Unusual place-setting pieces also get the premium, particularly oyster/cocktail/seafood forks; pie forks and ice cream spoons; round cream soup spoons and bouillon spoons, egg spoons, chocolate spoons, chocolate muddlers and orange spoons.

So dig up those old Rogers pieces that have been languishing in storage all these years, especially if they are interesting serving pieces. You're just a little bit of buffing away from a very classy buffet.

Moonlight In Denmark

This is what the Danish silversmith, Georg Jensen (1866-1935), said in an interview on the occasion of his 60th birthday in 1926:

"Silver is the best material we have. Gold is precious for its worth, not for its effect. Silver has that lovely glow of moonlight, something like the light of a Danish summer night. Silver is like the dusk, dewy and misty. Gold, on the other hand, is effective only in its brilliance and that conceals much."

True lovers of silver, like myself, will often compare it lyrically to moonlight. And that's true; the allure of silver is more in its romantic effect than in its monetary value.

But it can't be denied that some of the recent surge of interest in silver has been fueled by its dramatic increased in value.

Items made of silver, however, will always be valued for their artistry more than their weight, and this is especially true of Georg Jensen's silver, which lately has become more valuable than Tiffany's.

Georg Jensen was the son of a blacksmith. He went to work at the foundry at an early age, and at 14 years old apprenticed to a goldsmith.

He was an artist, however, who loved to draw and had ambitions to be a sculptor. So, when the time came, he applied to Royal Academy of

Fine Arts and was accepted. And when he graduated in 1892, he went to work as a potter.

Jensen married and had two children, but when his wife died he decided to go back to his roots in metal craft.

It was a decision that made sense. He had wanted to be a sculptor and had worked with metal since he was a child. Now he could sculpt silver, the metal he loved the most.

In 1904 Jensen opened a silver shop at 36 Bergrade in Copenhagen. By 1920, he was employing 250 workers and had outlets for his work around the world, including New York, London and Paris.

Jensen's success, and the reason his work is still so highly prized, lies in the labor-intensive quality of his pieces. He is universally recognized as the most talented and influential silver designer of the 20th Century.

His deceptively simple designs represent the best work of both the Arts and Crafts Movement and Modernism.

Jensen produced 33 different silver patterns, but the most famous in this country was his the simple and elegant "Acorn" pattern.

Acorn was so admired that International Silver produced an affordable knock-off pattern in the late1930s called "Royal Danish." By the post-war 1940s it became, and still remains, one of the top ten silver patterns ever produced in the United States.

Jensen marks include: either his name in script inside a crowned wreath, or a small "gj" next to its mirror image, a backward "jg," under a crown.

The Mexican Plateros

Silver is plentiful in Mexico and has been mined and crafted there as far back as pre-Columbian times.

After the Spanish conquests, it was the Mexican "plateros," or silver craftsmen (from the Spanish "plato," for silver), who taught the North American natives, like the Navajos, to make silver jewelry.

But the craze for Mexican silver during the mid-20th Century from 1930-1970 is generally said to have begun with two men from the United States, Frederick Davis and William Spratling.

In the mid-1920s Davis was working in Mexico City as the manager of a news company and supplementing his income by designing and crafting silver objects and jewelry for the tourist trade.

Eventually he got a job in the antiques and gifts shop at Sanborn's, a famous restaurant in the city that catered to American tourists. He sold his own unique designs in a shop next to Sanborn's, and before long the word hit the States that if you went to Mexico, you had to buy silver at Sanborns.

In 1927, a major road was completed between Mexico City and Acapulco. The road went right through the city of Taxco (also spelled Tasco), a major center in the Mexican silver trade.

It was to Taxco that William Spratling came in 1929 not long after graduating from Tulane with a degree in architecture.

Spratling was something of a Renaissance man. He wrote a book called "Little Mexico" and opened a gift shop on the Taxco road selling, among other things, his drawings of the local landscape and buildings.

He also opened a silver workshop employing local labor to execute his designs. He eventually named his shop "Taller Las Delicias" (The Workshop of Delights), and by 1940 it was employing 300 workers.

During World War II, Spratling took advantage of the lack of European exports to the U.S. and signed lucrative contracts with Nieman Marcus, Saks Fifth Avenue, Macy's and other retailers.

Spratling is called the Father of the Taxco School of silver craft, because so many of his employees went on to become independent designers.

It is estimated that there are currently nearly 10,000 silver craftsmen in Taxco today. Some of the old names to look for include: the Castillo Brothers, Antonio Pineda, Hector Aguilar, Margot van Vorhees Castillo, Matilde Poulat, Felipe Martinez, Salvado Teran, Sigi, Hubert Harmon, and Serafin Moctezuma, among others.

The appeal of Mexican sterling is in its wonderful combination of primitive, modern and traditional designs and its very generous silver weight. And why not? There's lots of it.

Copper Is Not Just Pennies Anymore

Copper is an element that naturally occurs in the earth. Archaeologists generally agree that copper and gold were the first metals known to man, and that their discovery was probably simultaneous.

Like gold, copper is a very soft element, but it is stronger than gold and more easily fashioned into useful shapes. Also, like gold, copper reflects the light, and it will not rust.

Copper can corrode, however, and although its natural color ranges from pink to brownish red, it can discolor over time with a green surface tint called "verdigris."

The word "verdigris" literally means "green of Greece," because it was the color of so many early Greek items made of bronze, an alloy of copper and tin. Brass is an alloy of copper and zinc.

In 1742, in Sheffield England, Thomas Boulsover discovered that silver and copper would bond inextricably at a certain temperature. This was the first silver plate, and to this day all silver plated copper is called Sheffield.

Most early American copper items were imported from England. But by the time of the Revolution, many American metalcrafters, including Paul Revere, were working with copper.

Copper is too soft to be cast in molds, so early copper is mostly handworked and joined with dovetailing. Larger dovetails were employed in the 1700s than in the 1800s. Industrial advances of the mid-1800s enabled copper to be rolled in sheets and joined without dovetailing.

Copper is a good conductor of electricity, which is why it is used in wiring. But it is also a good conductor of heat, which is why it was made into so many cooking vessels. Copper is still used in today's modern cookware.

Collectors of old copper—artistic, decorative and utilitarian—love the color and the craftsmanship, and a display of many pieces can be impressive. They also don't mind the polishing.

Although copper is easy to clean, and collectors love the soft patina it gets with age, it is okay to have copper items professionally lacquered without fear of losing antique value. This is particularly helpful in seaside areas, where copper items tarnish so quickly.

Commonly collected functional items in copper include tea kettles, coal scuttles, kitchen molds, bedwarmers, and trivets.

Really turning collectors' heads these days, however, are the decorative copper items produced during the Arts and Crafts era of the late 19th and early 20th Centuries:

By the way, silver is a by-product of copper. In fact, silver is rarely mined anymore. It is just extracted from the waste of the more industrially useful copper.

Those who follow metal prices in the newspapers can tell you how copper and silver prices will rise and fall together. These days, both are on the rise.

Mining For Old Aluminum

Here's a bit of trivia for all you Jeopardy fans out there:

The answer is—"The most abundant metallic element on earth."

And the winning question—"What is aluminum?"

It's also one of the most abundant metals you'll find in antique shops.

Aluminum comprises 8.13 percent of the earth's crust, making it the most abundant metallic element we have. But getting this element into a metallic form stumped scientists for centuries.

The original processes, first using potassium and then sodium, were so expensive that by the middle of the 19th Century, the price of aluminum was nearly $600 a pound.

In 1886 that price plummeted to about 60 cents a pound. That's when an American, Charles Hall, and a Frenchman, Paul Heroult, simultaneously invented an electrolytic reduction process that made metallic aluminum cheap and abundant.

As an inexpensive, lightweight, noncorrosive and extremely malleable metal, aluminum quickly found many industrial and utilitarian applications.

Today's collectors, however, are looking for the decorative and giftware aluminum made from the late 1920s until the mid-1950s.

Some of it was hand-hammered and much of it was machine-tooled.

Companies to look for include: Wendell August Forge, Arthur Amour, Continental Silver Company, Everlast, Palmer-Smith, DePoncea, Buenilum, Rodney Kent and Cellini Craft.

Collectors look for barware, like ice buckets, colorful tumblers, coasters, cocktail shakers and beverage trays.

Actually, all sorts of trays were made of aluminum, and some people look for special patterns, like Continental's "Chrysanthemum" or Rodney Kent's "Tulip."

Aluminum items were popular as wedding and shower gifts during the Depression years. Look for napkin holders, bread trays, trivets, centerpiece bowls and baskets.

Aluminum can get dull and dirty with age. Collectors recommend automotive wheel polish or a simple all-metal cleaner like Simichrome.

Nobody collects aluminum as an investment, but rather because it's interesting, fun and inexpensive. Most items are priced anywhere from a couple of dollars to about $35.

Here's some more aluminum trivia:

Aluminum gets its name because it is a base element in alum, the stuff styptic sticks are made of. Sometime later it was given the traditional "-ium" ending as a member of the Table of Elements. "Aluminium" stuck as the British pronunciation for decades, but these days everyone has reverted just to saying "aluminum."

Cameos, The Heirloom Jewelry

There is an heirloom quality about a cameo that few other items of jewelry possess. Even if you have just purchased one, as soon as you put it on it looks like something that has been handed down for generations.

This is probably because cameos are among the oldest forms of man-made jewelry, dating back to ancient Greece. Their classical origins made them extremely popular during the Renaissance of the 15th and 16th Centuries, and again during the neoclassical revival of the 18th Century.

Technically, a cameo is a decoration in relief. The opposite of a cameo, and actually predating it, is the intaglio, where the decoration is recessed—carved into the material rather than on it.

Over the centuries, cameos have been created on various materials—semi-precious stones like onyx, agate, jet and beryl, as well as lava rock, ivory, coral, amber and, most commonly, shell.

They have also been made of wax, glass, gutta-percha (a resinous sap), glass, celluloid, Bakelite and a variety of plastics.

In the late 18th Century, two new kinds of cameos made their appearance in Great Britain. The Scotsman, James Tassie, developed the "Tassie" cameo of glass paste, cast in a hand carved mold. And the Staffordshire potter, Josiah Wedgwood, created cameo jewelry from his famous stoneware ceramic called Jasperware.

It is the huge popularity of cameos in the 19th Century, however, that has made them the staple of the antique jewelry market that they are today.

At the beginning of the century, Napoleon's wife, Josephine, wore a crown studded with cameos at her husband's coronation. She also popularized the cameo "parure" set: matching earrings, necklace, brooch, bracelet and ring. Napoleon presented her with such a set containing eighty-two cameos adorned with 275 pearls.

The cameo was also a favorite of Queen Victoria, and she loved giving them as gifts. Wearing a cameo in London at the time was like saying you had been to see the Queen.

A cameo might also indicate that you were wealthy enough to have gone on a "grand tour" abroad, a trip to the classical sights of Greece and Italy meant to round off one's education. One of the most popular grand tour souvenirs from Italy were carved shell cameos and those created out of the lava rock of Mt. Vesuvius in Pompeii.

The French created a "cameo habille," or dressed-up cameo, where the figure in the cameo is wearing jewelry, usually a necklace or earring made of mine-cut diamonds or diamond chips.

It even became popular in the 19th Century for men to sport cameos, usually as rings, watch fobs or ascot pins. The figures on these were often classical warriors, with Caesar and Alexander the Great as the leading examples.

Cameos have also been carved with flowers as well as scenes depicting historical or biblical events. Rebecca at the Well was a favorite.

The female figures on early cameos were usually specific mythological personalities—The Bacchante: a plump-faced, wild-haired follower of the god Bacchus was popular, along with Juno, Venus, Demeter, Diana, the three Graces or any one of the nine muses.

By the mid-19th Century the female figures were more generalized and often wore the popular hairdos of the day. By around 1900, the classical, aquiline nose was traded for the more fashionable, pert and perky, upturned nose—more Gibson girl than goddess.

It is at this point in time, the turn of the century, that cameos became the victim of their own popularity. To fill the demand for cameos, craftsmen began knocking them out with little attention to detail. To make them more affordable, base metals replaced gold, silver and platinum in the settings, and plastic costume cameos were produced in abundance.

The most valuable cameos are those made before 1850, those with additional jewels in the setting, and Grand Tour lava cameos, usually carved with great detail in very high relief.

Whatever the age of your cameo and whatever material it is made from, it looks like an heirloom. So wear it as proudly as an heir or heiress.

The Magic Of Gemstones

The value of gems is determined by their relative hardness and rarity. There are only four precious gems: diamond, sapphire, ruby and emerald. All the rest are called semiprecious.

Jewelry has also been made from other natural substances that are technically not gems, like amber (tree sap), tortoise, corral, ivory, bone, pearl and mother of pearl (seashell).

But the lure of gems is the lore about gems, the real reason why so much fabulous jewelry has been made with them. These substances have so mesmerized the human race that over the centuries people have ascribed significance to them far beyond their monetary value.

Gemstones have long been associated with beauty, power and wealth, but people have also believed them to have mystical or curative powers. Even in our own modern, sophisticated times, ordinary crystals are touted by some as having amazingly positive effects on the human heart and soul.

Both the Old and New Testaments contain references to gemstones having mystical symbolism. In Exodus 28: 17-20, the breastplate of the high priest of Jerusalem is described as being set with twelve jewels. The tradition is that these jewels, each inscribed with an anagram for the name of God, represent the twelve tribes of Israel.

The Hebrew names for these stones are differ from our own, but scholars have figured them to line up this way : Ruben (carnelian), Simeon (peridot), Levy (emerald), Judah (garnet), Issachar (lapis lazuli), Zebulon (rock crystal), Joseph (zircon), Benjamen (agate), Dan (amethyst), Naphtali (citrine), Gad (onyx), and Asher (jasper).

The walls of the city of New Jerusalem are described by St. John in Revelations 21: 19-21 as bearing the names of the twelve Apostles, and adorned with twelve jewels. That list lines up this way: Peter (jasper), Andrew (sapphire), James the Greater (chalcedony), John (emerald), Philip (sardonyx), Bartholomew (sard), Matthew (chrysolite), Thomas (beryl), James the Lesser (topaz), Jude (chrysoprase), Simon (hyacinth), and Judas (amethyst).

Since the Bible seemed to be associating different stones with different personalities, so certain gems became associated with people born under different signs of the Zodiac: Aquarius (garnet), Pisces (amethyst), Aries (bloodstone), Taurus (Sapphire), Gemini (agate), Cancer (emerald), Leo (onyx), Virgo (carnelian), Libra (chrysolite), Scorpio (aquamarine), Sagittarius (topaz), and Capricorn (ruby).

These zodiacal gems gave rise to the idea of birth stones. Most people today can tell you their birth stone: January (garnet), February (amethyst), March (aquamarine or bloodstone), April (diamond), May (emerald), June (pearl, moonstone or alexandrite), July (ruby), August (peridot or sardonyx), September (sapphire), October (opal), November (topaz or citrine) and December (turquoise or zircon).

During the Middle Ages and the Renaissance, scholars further speculated about these groups of twelve by attributing various powers to the stones based on their biblical associations.

These gemstones were theorized to have power over the twelve hierarchies of the devil, the twelve angels mentioned in scripture and the twelve choirs of angels, as well as having curative effects on twelve parts of the human anatomy.

Some gems even get their names from the curative powers attributed to them. Jade, for instance, which was supposed to cure disorders of the kidney, gets its name from the Spanish, *piedras de ijada,* meaning "stones for the side." The word amethyst is from the Greek meaning "against intoxication."

Wealthy Romans routinely swallowed pearls for health, a practice they picked up from the Egyptians. Amber was long considered a cure for stomach disorders. Sapphire was used to cure boils and malachite as a local anesthetic.

All of the superstitions concerning the mystical and medicinal properties of gemstones had been debunked by the early 1600s, but, as with the crystal today, people just can't resist believing there is something more to these glittering and colorful stones.

It's Tole For Thee

Tole, hand-painted metalwork, has long been a favorite of antiquers. As time goes by, and much of the good old tole becomes rarer and more expensive, collectors seem to find new, more available and affordable varieties.

The term "tole" comes from the French word for sheet iron, but tole ware may be any sheet metal, usually tin. Technically, the term in French for hand-painted tin is *tole peinte*, but we just call it tole.

You may also hear the British term "pontypool" (or "pontipool wares") used to describe old decorated tin. This word comes from the city of Pontypool in Wales, where the technique originated with the Allgood family, who started the Pontypool Japan Works in 1725.

"Japanning" is the term used for decorating any black, orange, red or dark brown lacquered surface with enamel. The technique has been used on wood furniture, picture frames and boxes, but is particularly practical on metal wares as a rust retardant.

The British continued to produce pontypool ware, most notably in Birmingham and in Wolverhampton (Staffordshire) throughout the 18th and 19th Centuries. Most of the decorations were English or Oriental in design. By the late 19th Century, demand became so great that the tole was often mass-produced with stencil designs

English pontypool boxes became a rage throughout Europe during the early 1900s, and were reproduced in comparable quality by the Georg Sobwasser firm in Braunsweig, Germany. The French produced fine tole wares during the period of the Looeys (Louis XIV, V and VI) prior to the French Revolution. Some of the most exquisite *tole peinte*, however, was made during the Napoleonic empire period (1790-1815). Empire tole is most often decorated with classical (Greek and Roman) motifs.

Tole ware in America dates back to the colonial tinsmiths before the American Revolution. They were mostly located in New England, notably in Connecticut, and in New York State. By the mid-19th Century, however, tole-ware production became the province of the Pennsylvania Dutch, who continued it up through the Depression Era of the 1930s.

Pennsylvania Dutch tole is what has most often been sought after by local antiquers. Designs on these pieces are very distinctive—usually geometric or with stylized foliage and flowers.

Some less expensive mid-20th Century tole has become very collectible today. Look for pieces from the 1930s through the 1950s decorated with hand-painted floral designs.

Never Go Walking Out
Without Your Hat Pin

"Never go walking out without your hat pin.

It's about the best protection you have got.

For if you go walking out without your hat pin,

You may come home without your you-know-what."

As this bawdy English music hall song from the turn of the century suggests, hatpins could be useful to women in all sorts of ways. In fact, those pins became quite liberating. You might say that modern women's history begins with big hats and the long pins necessary to keep them in place.

Around 1850 women throughout Europe and America began shedding their lowly bonnets in favor of large elaborate hats that helped them stand out in a crowd and assert their personalities.

These hats required hatpins, some as long as 10 to 14 inches, and before long the design of the pins became as important as the hats themselves.

The most beautifully designed hatpins were made in France, and Victorian ladies just had to have them.

In fact, and I'm not making this up, the demand for French hatpins in England became so great that it upset the balance of trade between the two countries. This forced Parliament to pass an act, limiting the sale of hatpins to only two days a year in early January.

As a result, women would save money all year long, often by scrimping on their household allowance, in order to buy their pins come January. Thus, we get the term, "pin money," as money put aside for a personal indulgence.

This particular series of events helped prove women's economic strength, an important factor in achieving political equality. But the hatpin had still more work to do. Hatpins soon became a symbol of women's power.

Just as that musical hall song was becoming popular, antifeminists in the British judiciary decided that hatpins were potential weapons, and banned them from courtrooms and from the demonstrations of suffragettes. In 1914 several suffragettes were arrested in Perth, England, for wearing hatpins in their hats.

Collectors today may collect hatpins for their beauty and craftsmanship, but they also realize their importance in one of the most significant 20th Century advances in democracy.

A collection of genuine hatpins from the 1850s to the 1930s can be very impressive. While many were made with precious jewels and metals, most were created in artfully designed settings of semiprecious gems, colored glass and rhinestones.

Most hatpins are not marked in any way except if they have gold or silver content. The most frequently found maker's mark is an intertwined "CH" for Charles Horner, a prolific creator of hatpins in the late 19th Century in Halifax, Canada.

While a few old hatpins can costs thousands, most are not nearly that pricey and you are bound to find some bargains here and there.

The era of hatpins is 1850 to 1930, and the same is true for hatpin holders. Like hatpins, the holders can be found in a variety of materials from art glass to silver, but most holders were created in porcelain. The most sought-after of these are marked Nippon, Royal Bayreuth, Limoges or R.S. Prussia.

Chasing After Chase

When the United States was asked to participate in the groundbreaking decorative arts exhibition in Paris in 1925, the exhibit that gave Art Deco its name, then Interior Secretary Herbert Hoover declined, saying there was "no modern decorative art movement in America."

The statement wasn't exactly true. There were many artists and designers working in the modern style and some of them were collaborating. In fact, when a group of American designers visited the Paris exhibition, they came back convinced that modern design in the U.S. was even more advanced than in Europe.

The problem in this country, however, was that designers had not been getting together with manufacturers. But the embarrassing scandal of Hoover's remark lit a spark, and by 1930 many American manufacturers had hired modern designers to come up with new product ideas.

One of these companies was the Chase Brass and Copper Company of Waterbury, Connecticut, which opened its Specialty Sales Division in 1930, just to produce modern-style objects for the home.

To accomplish this, the company hired some of the finest designers in America—Helen Bishop, Rockwell Kent, Russel Wright and Walter Von Nessen, just to name a few.

Chase had been founded as the Waterbury Manufacturing Company by August S. Chase in 1876. From that time until it opened the specialty division, the company made only the brass parts of things—components of other objects. Its first patent, for instance, was an umbrella tip, and by the early 20th Century, the company boasted of producing 33,000 brass components for all sorts of useful, everyday objects.

It was from this inventory of commercial components that the Chase designers ingeniously created an array of decorative objects.

Elbow joints, for instance, became their famous cat and horse bookends; a wide chrome pipe became a coffee pot; smaller chrome pipes were reinvented into bud vases; and the hollow copper toilet tank floater was turned into several different items: the Chase "Glow Lamp," a "Victorian" vase, and a syrup jug, among other things.

A wide variety of Chase items are still relatively inexpensive compared to most vintage Art Deco items. Some Chase pieces do command a premium, including electric coffee urns, bookends, pairs of candlesticks, cocktail sets, and smoke stands.

The Chase mark is the Centaur, a mythological archer who is half man and half horse, along with the name CHASE or CHASE USA. It may be a hard mark to find. It is not always on the bottom of a piece, but may appear on a screw or rivet head, a handle or in a groove in the design.

In 1942, Chase closed down its Specialty Sales Division to return to making components, this time under government contract to manufacture metal parts for war-related items. The company is still in the components business in Montpelier, Ohio.

Chase specialty designs (1930-1942) do nothing less than define American Art Deco style, perhaps even more than the hotels of Miami's South Beach, because Chase products made their way into so many everyday middle-class homes across this country. They are also a testament to how good old-fashioned American ingenuity was able to adapt itself to modern living.

The standard price guides still list Chase as being quite inexpensive. Perhaps part of the reason is that so many of their products celebrate smoking and drinking, activities certainly more glamorized in the mid-20th Century than they are today.

That's part of Chase's charm, however. It truly evokes its time, especially its vigor and forward-looking imagination. Whatever the vices of that time, we could sure use a dose of it today

The Man Who Wouldn't Give Waltham The Time

The world of antiques is a world of stories, and many of these stories prove to us how nothing was ever produced in a vacuum. Each of the items you see in an antique shop is a product of its times and the personalities involved in producing it.

A case in point is the American Watch Company of Waltham, Massachusetts, better known as simply "Waltham," the company that dominated American watchmaking for nearly one hundred years from the 1850s until the 1950s.

Waltham was the brainchild of Aaron L. Dennison, a watchmaker, who conceived of a process for mass-producing pocket watches with interchangeable parts.

This was a new idea in 1857. Up to that time each watch was created, like an item of jewelry, as a unique piece with parts made especially for it.

The investing public was skeptical of Dennison's idea, but he found a believer in a local businessman with the daunting name of Royal Elisha Robbins.

After initial bankruptcy, Robbins reorganized the company in 1859, and thus began a battle of wills between him and Dennison.

Robbins took a conservative approach, slimming down the work-force and asking those who remained to work for half wages. He limited production and held back the introduction of new models.

Dennison, on the other hand, was eager to see his idea come to fruition as soon as possible. He chafed under Robbins' reforms and felt frustrated that he was no longer in control of an idea he believed once belonged to him alone.

Dennison was particularly miffed that Robbins refused to support the production of an inexpensive watch ($15-18) and vigorously market it to soldiers fighting the Civil War.

The conflict between the two got so bad that in 1862 the company reluctantly fired Dennison, the man whose idea had created the company in the first place.

Dennison sued, and he received a settlement of $5,000 and a fairly lucrative contract to produce watch cases. But if he had patiently held on, and put up with Robbins' reforms for just a few more years, he would have become a very, very rich man.

While Dennison's idea for the military watches was probably a good one and could have been a moneymaker, the company under Robbins' conservative leadership went on to become America's premier watch company.

Waltham was honored at the 1876 American Centennial Exhibition in Philadelphia, and particularly impressed the Swiss member of the international jury that judged the watch competition.

He declared, in a speech to Swiss watchmakers back home, that Waltham was proof that American machine-made watches with interchangeable parts looked better and worked better than any other watches he had seen. He predicted that the United States would become "the leading watch-producing nation in the world."

He was right. By the turn of the century, Waltham had grown so big that it built a village for its workers to live in and started up its own trolley service to bring the workers to and from their jobs.

Waltham watches are among the most collectible watches on today's antiques market. Prices range from a hundred dollars to the sky's the limit. Watches with lower serial numbers, from the Civil War and before, are particularly valuable, as are those with very fancy or solid gold cases.

Here's some more watch lore.

Sometime in the late 1800s, the story goes, a French watchmaker noticed a woman on a park bench nursing her child. For convenience, she had wrapped a pocket watch around her wrist. The watchmaker was so struck by the practicality of the idea that he set about making a "bracelet watch."

The French were the earliest manufacturers of wristwatches, but the concept just didn't fly in the rest of the world, especially not among the

English, who thought the idea of a man wearing a bracelet of any kind was just too ... well, too French.

The Swiss made watch-wearing manly, when they marketed wrist-watches to soldiers fighting World War II. After the war, the wrist-watch overtook the pocket watch in popularity.

Fabulous Fakes With Real Names

There are two very real names behind the fact that fake jewelry became such a phenomenon in the 20th Century. One was a manufacturer, the other a designer.

The manufacturer was Daniel Swarovski, a Bohemian glassmaker, who in 1891 invented a machine that could mass-produce polished glass gems into precisely cut designs.

As a result, virtually all the cut glass, crystal and colored, made for costume jewelry in the early 20th Century was produced in Bohemia, which, after 1918, became part of Czechoslovakia.

It was the French fashion designer, Gabrielle (Coco) Chanel, however, who made it chic for women everywhere and on every level of society to sport fake baubles.

Chanel had one guiding principle about costume jewels. "It doesn't matter if they are not real," she proclaimed in 1924, "as long as they look like junk."

Since costume jewels didn't have to look like traditional jewels, they could look like anything. That let designers free to be more imaginative.

Also, since costume jewels were inexpensive, you could toss them aside as fads changed and buy new jewelry to suit the current fashion. This is why old costume jewels truly evoke the time in which they were made.

The height of costume jewelry production spans the forty years from the mid-1920s through the 1960s. It was a time of rapid changes in fashion that really challenged the designers.

Here are the names of some of the designers and manufacturers who rose to the occasion:

Elsa Schiaparelli was a fashion designer and contemporary rival of Chanel. She incorporated faux jewels into her fashion designs, especially the buttons, where she used faux pearls and rhinestones.

Albert Weiss began as a designer for the Coro company and then started his own firm in 1942. He chose the very best glass gems, both clear and in the most beautiful colors, and had them cut to perfection. The butterfly was one of his favorite motifs.

The Eisenberg family first made a name for itself selling ready-to-wear women's clothing in Chicago at the turn of the century. One of their signatures was to grace each piece with a brilliant rhinestone pin from the Swarovski company.

By the 1930s they were in the jewelry business themselves, selling rhinestones set in sterling. Their big hit was the "Eisenberg Ice" line, with rhinestones set in rhodium, introduced in 1950.

If you have inherited or accumulated masses of costume jewels, don't be so quick to toss them aside. Take some time with a magnifying glass or a jeweler's loupe to see if any of those gorgeous old gewgaws are marked. If they are, your fabulous fakes could be worth some real money.

Clean costume jewels gingerly, being careful not to soak or submerge them. Moisture can loosen the setting or get trapped in the foil-back rhinestones and discolor them. Trapped moisture will also be a problem if you store them in sealed plastic bags. Use jewelry pouches or plain tissue paper.

Other real names to look for on costume jewelry include: Trifari, Hobe, Ciner, Emmons, Kenneth Jay Lane, Robert, Panetta, Mobe, Dior, Simpson, St. Laurent, Cardin, Klein, Kramer, Coro, Jolle, Schreiner and others.

The stories about Hattie Carnegie and Miriam Haskell are so special they deserve a chapter all their own.

Beauty Was Their Business

The two most powerful forces in mid-20th Century American fashion were women, both of whom were born in the late19th Century.

The stories of Hattie Carnegie and Miriam Haskell are as dazzling and inspiring as the creations they would become famous for.

It's hard for us to comprehend just how much influence Hattie Carnegie wielded over American fashion in the late 1920s and early '30s.

There was the "Little Carnegie Suit" for women in the workplace and for dinner out and the theater, the "Carnegie Look," a simple, stylish and understated ensemble that often included a cape or stole.

Carnegie also designed furs, hats, lingerie, perfumes, bags and other accessories including, of course, her famous costume jewelry, which has now become so collectible.

On March 15, 1886, Hattie Carnegie was born in Vienna, Austria, as Henrietta Helen Koningeiser. In German, the "o" has two dots over it (an umlaut), so the name was pronounced sort of like "Kanengieser," which is the way it was spelled in America, where Hattie grew up on the lower east side of Manhattan.

As a young woman, she went to work at Macy's as a model. It was common at the time for the department store to employ "live mannequins," not only in the store windows, but also modeling fashions while walking the aisles in the store.

In 1909, Hattie partnered with her friend Rose Roth, a seamstress, to open a dress shop. They designed and made their own versions of European styles, adapting them to simpler American tastes. The company enjoyed some success, but Hattie had bigger ideas.

In 1918, Carnegie bought out her partner and struck out on her own. She expanded the company's line of products, and chose the name Carnegie, because it represented wealth and status.

The risk paid off in 1925 when the prestigious California department store, I. Magnum, picked up her line. The "Hattie Carnegie look" on Broadway and Hollywood stars soon became a sensation from coast to coast.

Carnegie was a petite woman, only four feet nine inches tall and never more than 100 pounds, but she was a commanding and demanding business woman.

"Beauty is my Business" was her slogan in the fashion magazine ads and by the time she passed away in 1956, that business was worth $8 million—an enormous fortune for the time.

To learn more, get the new book, "Hattie Carnegie Jewelry: Her Life and Her Legacy," by Georgina McCall. Or check out the adoring and comprehensive web site: Hattie-Carnegie.com.

Born in 1899, over twenty years before American women got the right to vote, Miriam Haskell would be called, "The First Lady of American Fashion" in the 1930s and '40s and one of the leading business women of her day.

As a teenager she worked in her father's business in Albany, Indiana. Always an independent girl, she set out for New York in her early twenties and found a job at a gift shop in the McAlpin Hotel in fashionable Herald Square.

It was there that she got the idea to start her own business making costume jewelry, a relatively new market in those days.

In 1924, with an initial investment from her father, Haskell opened a store on West 57th Street selling handmade costume jewelry in her own designs. Then she set about wearing those jewels around town.

Slender and pale with dark hair and eyes, Miriam became the perfect model for her own wares. She dressed glamorously, spoke intelligently and hobnobbed in all the right places.

In effect Miriam Haskel became for New York what Coco Chanel and Elsa Schiaparelli had become for Paris—an arbiter of elegant taste and a symbol of the independent woman.

In 1933 she moved her shop to 392 Fifth Avenue, definitely a step-up. Betty Grable's famous World War II pinup poster, with her upswept hair, made Miriam Haskel's faux tortoise, faux pearl and rhinestone side combs popular.

Before long Haskell had expanded her business to several floors at that tony Fifth Avenue address, where the business would remain until the late 1960s.

At the Stork Club or at Twenty-One, on the arm of Bernard Gimbel or Nelson Rockefeller, Haskel sold her jewelry with her celebrity. Parties at her home on Central Park South or in her suite at the St. Moritz were always fodder for the society columns.

As an unmarried and powerful woman in a male-dominated business, however, she was often the object of dark rumors.

It was said, for instance, that, after she turned over the business to her brother Joseph in the late 1960s, she lived out her life as a sour old spinster and died in poverty.

None of that is true. Miriam spent a restful retirement among family and friends until she died in 1981, two days after her 82nd birthday.

To learn more about Miriam Haskel, and to see wonderful color photos of her magnificent legacy of artful jewelry designs, read "Fifty Years of Collectible Fashion Jewelry: 1925-1975" by Lillian Baker.

PART VI

Stories About Books
And Prints

Hitting The Books On Old Books * The Mysterious Creator(s) Of Nancy Drew * The Illustrious Currier And Ives * Bessie Pease Gutman * The Dreamy Art Of Maxfield Parrish * Wallace Nutting: The Minister Of Beauty * Fred Thompson Fred Thompson * The Comics: A Century Of Toons

Hitting The Books On Old Books

Of all the items we may have inherited or accumulated over the years, old books cause us the most confusion when it comes time to dispose of them.

If you are not an antiquarian (the technical term for a collector or dealer in old books), it's hard to tell what books are valuable and what to put out in the yard sale for a dollar.

The truth is that most old books are just used books and have little value at all. But the market for old books has been very active lately, so it's always best to check through your pile first, especially if the books were handed down to you.

Among the books antiquarians hit while doing their job is "Bookman's Price Index," a yearly guide to book prices. It's an expensive book, so if you are not in the business, you may want to use the library's copy.

Beginners, however, can own a copy of "Huxford's Old Book Value Guide" (Collector Books), which lists about 25,000 of the most sought-after collectibles.

A very important guide in the business is the comprehensive "A Guide to First Editions" by Edward Zempel and Linda Verklen, published by Spoon River. This book contains statements from publishing houses about how, if at all, they indicated a first edition.

Every publishing house marked their first editions differently. There was no standard in the industry. And discovering whether or not you own a first edition can be important these days, because literary first editions are among the most collectible books on today's market.

This is especially true with 20th Century American authors. A first edition of Hemingway's "For Whom The Bell Tolls," for instance, can be over $2,500, and over $15,000 if it is signed.

Confusing the issue are the "reprint houses," publishing companies that exclusively or primarily publish reprints of old books rather than original titles.

If you intend to get involved in collecting first editions, it's best to get to know the names of these reprint publishers—like Grosset and Dunlop, L. L. Burt, Hearst, and others—or you may think you have a first edition, when you don't.

Book club editions are also less valuable, even when they state they are first editions. Cheaply produced and different in size from the publishers' originals, they are not quite real books, in the opinion of antiquarians, who put them in a category just slightly better than old paperbacks.

Other currently popular collectible books include: nonfiction books on Western Americana, war, particularly the Civil War, books on sports, especially golf, books on geography, architecture, fashion and, of course, old children's books.

The market in children's books is for just about anything from the pre-1950s. Of course, 19th Century children's books and school primers can be among the most valuable. However, there is an increasingly strong market for old "Dick and Jane" readers, Wonder Books, Golden Books and other baby-boomer books.

Miniature books, a popular novelty from the 1820s to the 1880s, are also good sellers today. The reason is probably the same now as then—they make great gifts. You wouldn't think such tiny books could be worth so much, but by contrast, large family bibles and sets of encyclopedias are rarely worth anything.

The few bibles with value are those published in America before 1800 (there are about ninety-five of them in existence), and those with extensive genealogy pages, where family births, marriages and deaths were recorded.

Good quality leather-bound sets of encyclopedias from the 19th Century are sold by antiquarians solely for their decorative value. The price to an interior designer may be around $20 a foot.

Interior decorators are paying more than ever for beautifully bound and illustrated home-library sets of famous authors. Good limited-edition sets from the turn of the century can fetch several hundred dollars, depending on the author, illustrator, quality of the binding and the condition.

Here are some books you might hope to find in your pile (Prices are current as of press time and are only used to show relative value): Jack Kerouac's *On the Road*, 1957 signed first edition ($42,000); John Steinbeck's *The Grapes of Wrath*, 1939 first edition ($4,800); Ian Fleming's *Casino Royale* (the first James Bond novel), 1953 first edition ($21,000); F. Scott Fitzgerald's *Tender is the Night*, 1934 first edition with original dust jacket, ($17,500); Nathaniel Hawthorne's *The Scarlet Letter*, 1850 first edition ($8,500).

The Mysterious Creator(s) Of Nancy Drew

Melanie Rehak in her recently published book, "Girl Sleuth: Nancy Drew and the Women Who Created Her" (Harcourt), writes, "The stories themselves are secondary, what we remember most is Nancy."

I think that's true of most great fictional detectives—Sherlock Holmes, Hercule Poirot, Sam Spade, Jessica Fletcher, et al.

The title of Ms. Rehak's book aside, however, the character of 16-year-old Nancy Drew was technically not created by a woman, or women, but by a gentleman from New Jersey, Edward Stratemeyer.

Stratemeyer, who also created the Bobbsey Twins, the Hardy Boys and Tom Swift, was born in Elizabeth on October 4, 1862 and died on May 10, 1930 in Newark.

His death came just 12 days after the first Nancy Drew books appeared, three volumes in a boxed set.

Stratemeyer was something of a genius when it came to inventing characters and plots. He started writing and publishing juvenile fiction right out of high school. The story is that he used to create stories on the back of the wrapping paper in his parents tobacco shop.

In his lifetime he would publish 160 books, 60 of them under his own name.

He would also write the outlines for 800 more books, as head of the Stratemeyer Literary Syndicate which he founded in New York in 1906.

Stratemeyer hired writers, gave them a list of characters and an outline, and let them go at it. Most of his books were published by Grosset & Dunlap.

For Nancy Drew, he hired Mildred Wirt Benson (née Mildred Augustine), the first woman to graduate with a master's degree in journalism from the University of Iowa. She would be paid $125 per book.

There would eventually be 56 Nancy Drew novels published right through the 1950s. Since Stratemeyer died after the first three, the rest would be created and written by Benson and Stratemeyer's daughter, Harriet, who ran the syndicate until her death in 1982.

Over the years Harriet and Mildred created a Nancy who was smart, persevering, confident and independent. Undoubtedly that was Stratemeyer's original intention, but it was these women who made it happen.

It has become quite the popular thing to decorate a child's room with these books, especially if they were favorites of the parents in their youth.

If you've never read them, you might be tempted to pick a few up to read to a child while enjoying the stories yourself.

Those who think Nancy Drew books are just for kids, consider this:

The same week I read a review of Melanie Rehak's book on Nancy Drew, I read this quote from the lead detective in a new mystery novel I was reading:

"It might sound childish, I know, but ever since I first encountered Nancy Drew at the age of nine or ten I've been fascinated by secret passages and the like."

The detective goes on to recall Nancy shivering her way through a hidden staircase in the old Turnbull mansion.

It seems that even some seventy-five years after his death, Stratemyer is still creating plots for writers.

The Illustrious Currier & Ives

The story of Currier and Ives begins in 1828, when 15-year-old Nathaniel Currier walked into Pendleton of Boston, one of America's oldest and most respected print shops, to begin his apprenticeship.

Currier was a fast learner. Just six years later, in 1834, he moved to New York City to begin his own business at 137 Broadway. The next year he moved to Number 1 Wall Street and the following year he opened two shops, one on Nassau Street and one on Spruce Street.

It was out of disaster, however, that Currier's big break came. On January 13, 1840, the steamboat *Lexington* burst into flames and was destroyed, killing most of the 140 passengers and crew on board.

Three days later Currier's finely drawn illustration of the event appeared, in all its horrific detail, in *The Extra Sun*, making Currier, at only 27-years-old, a national sensation.

In 1852, with Currier's business rapidly expanding, he took on extra help, including James Merritt Ives, an in-law of his brother, Charles. Ives and Currier got along so well that they eventually became partners, building on Currier's initial success to create the most enormously popular print house in American history.

Currier and Ives succeeded by giving the public an image of its own times. It was the lesson Currier learned with the *Lexington*: find out what the people would like to see, and give it to them in more minute detail then they ever could have imagined.

The heart of the 19th Century is chronicled in these prints: the Mexican war, the Civil War, the westward migration, the building of the railroads, the majesty of steamships and clipper ships.

They also depicted scenes of everyday life in their America: people at play, hunting and fishing, working; life in the cities, on the farm and on the prairie.

These are outdoor scenes, full of action and energy, capturing like a snapshot a frozen moment in time.

The secret to Currier and Ives's success was that they made their prints available to the maximum number of people. Sold by an army of street vendors and door-to-door peddlers throughout the country, small black and white prints cost as little as six cents and large color lithographs were only three dollars.

During the life of their business, Currier and Ives produced 10 million prints of over 7 thousand titles. Volume sales and a money-saving technology that didn't sacrifice quality helped them to keep the cost of their products down.

Nathaniel Currier retired in 1880 and died in 1888. Ives ran the business until his death in 1895. Sons of both the men continued the business until it closed in 1907.

Authentic Currier and Ives prints are still quite affordable, with many small prints available in the $100 to $350 price range. Some large prints are valued from $1,500 up to about $5,000.

Initial purchases should be made from reputable dealers, so collectors can familiarize themselves with the real thing—color tone and sheen, thickness of the paper and plate size.

Happily, most reproductions will be indicated as such on the bottom of the print. These have also become collectible in the $50 to $100 range.

Collectors also find it fun to look for Currier and Ives designs on dishes, glassware, spice jars and canisters, towels and napkins. Particularly collectible these days is the "Currier Ives" pattern of dinnerware made by Royal China in the 1950s.

Bessie Pease Gutman

The period 1890 to 1925 is considered the Golden Age of American Illustration Art. The magazine publishing business flourished during that time, chiefly due to new technology—high speed presses, improved coated paper, half-tone plates, and four-color printing—all making it possible to mass produce a high quality product inexpensively.

Most of the magazines produced, about 75 percent of them, were targeted at women.

The Women's Suffrage Movement was making women a political and economic force to be reckoned with. And the relative prosperity of the period had created a middle class with more leisure time, especially for the lady of the house.

Editors demanded illustrations that would appeal to women—fashion, home and family life, and especially, children. One artist who gave editors all that they wanted and more was Bessie Pease Gutman (1876-1960), particularly when it came to illustrations of infants, toddlers and young children.

Gutman became one of the most popular illustrators of her day, however, not only because she was an editor's dream, but because she was a good artist, well trained and prolific.

Gutman was a local girl of sorts, born in Philadelphia and raised in Mount Holly. Her talent was recognized early and while still in high school, a teacher sent one of her illustrations (a drawing of a young girl trying to catch a horse) to a Chicago exhibit, where it was accepted for display.

She began her formal training at the Philadelphia School of Design for Women (now the Moore College of Art), and moved on to become one of the first students to enter the New York School of Art, where she studied under the great American impressionist, William Merritt Chase.

While a member of the Art Students League, she met Bernhard Gutman, who with his brother Helmuth, started the Gutman and Gutman art publishing business in 1902. They asked Bessie to join them in their enterprise. She did, and eventually married Helmuth.

Gutman's extensive artistic training can be seen in her choice of color and command of light and shadow. But her true talent, in my opinion, is in her ability to capture real human character, even in her infants. So many illustrators fall into the trap of creating cartoonish caricatures.

Gutman not only created decorative prints and magazine art, she produced a wide array of postcards, calenders and advertising art from cereal boxes to department store newspaper ads. She also illustrated books, particularly children's books and those little "Baby Books," where a mother kept track of her infant's progress. All of her work is very collectible today.

Prices for American Illustration Art, especially from the Golden Age and the subsequent Art Deco era, have risen dramatically in the last decade and Gutman's work is no exception. Here are some examples. (Prices are quoted only to show relative value between prints and as of press time.)

Those of Gutman's prints (mostly 11-by-14-inches or 14-by-21-inches), that used to sell for about $50-75 are now selling for an average of $150-300.

Gutman's postcards range from $20 to $35; bookplates and color advertising art go for $225 to $500; magazine covers from $150 to $265.

There are some notable exceptions. "Poverty and Riches," a popular print featuring a wealthy woman with a dog and a poor woman with an infant is priced about $500. "When Daddy Comes Marching Home" (1919), showing a woman and her child on a balcony waving to the soldiers marching below, costs in the neighborhood of $1,200 to $1,500.

Her two rare depictions of black infants are particularly sought after. These are "Little Black Blew" (1906), $2,500 to $3,000; and "My Honey" (1926), $1,000 to $1,400.

There are also a couple of fairly rare Gutman nudes: "Symphony" ($250-400) and "Wood Magic" ($450-600), both published in 1921.

One of the bargains available in Gutman's works are her "Colonial" prints, produced in the 1930s to compete with the hand-colored photographs of Wallace Nutting. These are magnificently detailed interior scenes of women taking tea, doing household chores or tending to their children.

The neat thing about the Colonials is that they are all titled and signed in hand by the artist, unlike most of Gutman's prints where her signature is part of the print. Since most Gutman collectors prefer the prints of children, prices for the Colonials are in the $200 range, a modest sum considering their quality and the hand signature.

Old American decorative prints and illustrations have to be in good condition to maintain their value, and unfortunately, much of them aren't, because they were clumsily stored away in the attic or basement after they were no longer fashionable.

Restoration of this kind of artwork, if at all possible, can be costly, but well worth it if you know you can enjoy it now as much as they enjoyed it back then.

The Dreamy Art Of
Maxfield Parrish

In 1934, the artist and illustrator Maxfield Parrish wrote, "I am most happy in out-of-door things, subjects in nature's own light: fanciful things, in color and design, belonging to no particular time or place."

Throughout his lifetime, Parrish's illustrations were very much in demand, and even before he died at the age of ninety-five in 1966, his works had become highly collectible. His popularity was and is because his unique vision really captures our imagination.

So, how do "out-of-door things … in nature's own light" become "fanciful things … belonging to no particular time or place"?

One answer is in dreams, where everything seems so real but nothing is real at all.

Parrish's art is a dreamy art, and there are no nightmares. All the dreams are sweet dreams. And in a career that spanned two world wars, plus Korea and Vietnam, people were grateful for the occasional escape into Parrish's dreamworld.

Another place where the real meets the unreal is in the theater. Parrish's works always have a touch of the dramatic. This is especially true when he depicts people, but even in his landscapes the trees seem to be characters, actors playing a role.

Parrish's first job, at the age of twenty-six, was as the illustrator of the book, "Mother Goose in Prose," published in 1896. He would continue to illustrate books until 1925, with the publication of "Knave of Hearts." This combination of fiction and art seemed to lay the groundwork for a career of works blending romance and fantasy.

Other notable books illustrated by Parrish include: "The Arabian Nights, Their Best Known Tales" (1909); Washington Irving's "Knickerbocker's History of New York" (1900); Eugene Field's "Poems of Childhood" (1904); and Edith Wharton's "Italian Villas and Their Gardens" (1904).

In 1918 Parrish received one of the most important commissions of his career—to illustrate the yearly calendar tops for the Edison Mazda Division of General Electric. The challenge here was to show the effects of light. As a result, Parrish developed that special dreamy combination of light and color that would be his signature as an artist.

Parrish continued doing these calendars until 1934, and some people consider them the best work of his career. The calendars were produced in two basic sizes: large (18" x 37½") and small (8½" x 19").

These calendar illustrations were so beloved, that it became a common practice to keep them at year's end and have them framed. Some of the illustrations were cropped to fit in existing frames. This will seriously affect their resale value today, but the price range is still between $250 and $3,500 for a small, cropped to a large, uncropped print.

Some say Parrish's works seem like Art Nouveau, but some call them Art Deco. They are both and neither. The length of his career spanned both of these periods, and his works remain unique. You will notice this in such titles as: "Prometheus" (1920); "Spirit of the Night" (1919); "Enchantment" (1926) and "Venetian Lamplighter" (1924).

Throughout his career, Parrish had a long association with several of America's most popular magazines. He illustrated covers for such periodicals as *Colliers, Ladies Home Journal, Life, Harper's Weekly*, and *Century*. These magazine covers were often framed and today the originals (unframed) can fetch up to a couple of hundred dollars. The frames will add more, depending on their quality.

An artist as popular as Parrish was bound to be imitated and reproduced. Collectors usually divide reproductions into those produced during the artist's lifetime and the newer reproductions of the last thirty years.

The old reproductions or "period" reproductions are usually valued the same as the original Parrish works. Newer reproductions will be apparent to collectors by the slick finish and the heaviness of the paper and, to the truly wise, by the pattern of dots in the print revealed under a jeweler's glass.

Telltale signs of aging are also a clue to originals and period reproductions. Look for faded colors, yellow-brown patina on the print and on original backing paper. Better, buy your first Parrishes from reputable dealers, so you have something with which to compare future finds.

Generally, it is difficult to write about an artist's work without some illustration to refer to. But Parrish's works are such a part of the national consciousness, you will immediately recognize his style when you see it.

Parrish's works were also an intricate part of the material culture of his day. He illustrated playing cards, advertisements, posters, toys, games, children's books, greeting and post cards, match covers, menus, jigsaw puzzles and such commercial packaging as gelatin, chocolate, and cigar boxes.

Decoratively, Parrish prints work beautifully in bedrooms, bathrooms, stairwells, hallways, landings, alcoves, foyers, offices, libraries, and any place where a little dreamy fantasy or a touch of theater might provide a momentary escape to stimulate the imagination or brighten up your day.

Wallace Nutting—The Minister Of Beauty

In 1936, about five years before he died, Wallace Nutting said this:

"I am under no illusions as to my pictures. I am not an artist, and it is most disagreeable to me to be called one."

Nutting's "art"—hand-colored photographs of interior, exterior and foreign scenes—is perhaps the most ubiquitous on the antique market.

By his own company's account, there were over ten million of his works produced in his lifetime. Most of these were titled and signed in pencil, framed under glass in simple walnut frames, and sold inexpensively in department stores.

So if Nutting wasn't an artist, what was he?

"I am a clergyman with a love of the beautiful," he said, and the beautiful is what he gave us—idyllic country lanes, copses of flowering dogwood, cozy cottages limned with flowers, patterned gardens all in bloom, mountain lakes and streams.

Nutting was born in Rockbottom, Mass. on Sunday, November 17, 1861. Nine months later his father died in the Civil War.

He was brought up in Maine by his uncle, sent to Phillips Exeter, Harvard College and Union Theological. He eventually received his Doctor of Divinity from Whitman College in 1893 and practiced as a Congregationalist minister.

Citing ill health, he left the ministry in 1904, moved to New York City and opened the Wallace Nutting Art Print Studio on E. 23rd Street.

He would eventually set up shop in Southbury, CT. and Framingham. MA. At the height of his business, around 1912, when demand for his decorative photographs was greatest, he employed 200 colorists.

At any given time, only a handful of these artists, perhaps four or five, was authorized to title and sign the photographs. Nutting signed very few himself.

To learn more about Nutting signatures, including how to read them to date a piece, visit www.wallacenuttinglibrary.com on the Internet.

In 1912, Nutting began making reproductions of 18th Century English and Colonial furniture using original tools and techniques. He was so successful in recreating these pieces that unscrupulous dealers were removing his paper tags and selling the furniture as authentic antiques.

Nutting solved the problem by burning in a signature, first in script and later in plain block letters.

Nutting's pictures come in fifteen sizes from 4"x5" to 22"x28" and are priced accordingly from $50 to $300 for exterior scenes and from $75 to $600 from interior scenes.

Collectors like the staged interior scenes because they show interior furnishings and decoration as well as ladies' fashions.

No, they are not art and don't pretend to be; they are wall decorations. But they are also charming, warm, homey, honest, sensitive, nostalgic and sometimes quite beautiful—reason enough to proudly include them in your interior design.

Fred Thompson Fred Thompson

Lots of folks have old decorative prints in their attics and most of those prints aren't worth more than the frames they are in.

It might be a good idea to hold on to them, however, because you never know when collectors will start to re-discover some forgotten artist.

In the past, collectors have created exciting new markets for such American print-makers as Wallace Nutting, Maxfield Parrish, R. Atkinson Fox, Betsy Pease Gutmann, Harrison Fisher, David Davidson, Charles Sawyer and others. As a result, prices for the works of these artists have risen steadily over the years.

Recently, a great deal of attention is being paid to Fred Thompson prints, made in Portland, Maine, between 1908 and 1923.

The story is an interesting one of triumph and tragedy, and a legacy of fascinating artwork.

You will know a Thompson print by the distinctive "Fred Thompson" signature in elongated block letters, or by the a triangular label on the back, reading, "TACO" for Thompson Art Company.

What you may not know is that there are actually two Fred Thompsons, Frederick H. and Frederick M., father and son.

The senior Fred Thompson was born in Deering Center (now, Westbrook), Maine in 1844, the son of a minister.

From a young man, Fred's passion was for photography, but for practical reasons he went into the carriage making business with his older brother. It was called Zenas Thompson and Brother, and it went out of business in 1906 as automobiles became the wave of the future.

Still being practical, in 1907 Fred purchased a Portland restaurant called the Daisy Lunchroom and renamed it, "Thompson Spa," catering to tourists mostly from Boston.

Finally secure in his art, in 1908 he opened the Thompson Art Company, specializing in hand-colored photographs of New England landscapes and nature studies, which also catered to Maine tourists.

Influenced by the success of Wallace Nutting, who was 17 years his junior, Thompson also began photographing colonial-style interiors. Like Nutting, he filled a room in an old house with antiques and posed female models engaged in domestic chores.

Without a doubt, Thompson's photos of the Maine coastline, including those of tall ships and schooners, were his biggest sellers. His most popular piece was the Portland Head Lighthouse.

TAC was soon producing other souvenir items—calendars, trays, mirrors, greeting cards and paperweights—all with Thompson's prints on them.

Business was booming, and Thompson asked his son, Frederick M., a Tufts graduate in engineering, to help.

Some years later, on November 16, 1909, the senior Thompson committed suicide by ingesting cyanide. He was sixty-five, and it is presumed that the stresses of business had become too much for his naturally artistic temperament.

The younger Thompson continued the business until his death in 1923 at the age of forty-five.

Thompson prints are usually 5x7 inches or 16x20 inches and many of them can be found in the $50 to $150 price range. Some rare prints, however, can command from $150 to $300. Condition and framing are extremely important.

Most desirable are the nautical prints—the lighthouse, the sailing ships, and particularly, the "Old Pilot," a shot of a weathered old seaman with a white beard at the wheel of a ship, and "Toiler of the Sea," with the same seaman at the oars of a row boat.

There are as yet no known reproductions of Fred Thompson prints, which should make them very appealing not only to collectors but to anyone with a seaside property to decorate.

The Comics: A Century Of Toons

They have added such words to the dictionary as ZOWIE! SOCKO! and POW! They have given us the Dagwood sandwich and the Rube Goldberg contraption, and they foretold the cellular phone with Dick Tracy's "two-way wrist radio." They are popularly known as "the comics," or "the funnies," and they have been entertaining and influencing Americans for over a hundred years.

In 1895, artist Richard Outcault introduced a cartoon called "Hogan's Alley" for Joseph Pulitzer's New York daily, *The World*. The full-color comic featured a homely little boy in a yellow nightshirt known as the "Yellow Kid." He had a bald head and big ears, but his innocent gape was the perfect foil for poking fun at the foibles and pretensions of high society.

The Kid was such a huge success that William Randolph Hearst used his wealth to get the artist to draw the cartoon for *The Journal*, where it was renamed "The Yellow Kid," after its most loveable character. Two years later, in 1897, Hearst added Rudolph Dirk's "Katzenjammer Kids," the strip with the German accent, which still appears in some newspapers today, making it the world's longest running comic strip.

Some would argue that "Katzenjammer Kids" is actually the first strip, because it was the first to tell a story in a series of panels. "Yellow

Kid" was a single panorama cartoon with funny vignettes in every corner. One thing both these funnies had in common, however, was the use of balloon clouds for dialogue, which became a trademark for comic strips everywhere. In fact, the Italian word for comic strip is *fumetto,* little puff of smoke, named for the speech balloon.

Eventually, Hearst began publishing the first full-color funnies section—eight pages—in the *Morning Journal,* and the funny papers were on their way to becoming an American institution. The first daily black-and-white strip, "A. Piker, Clerk," appeared in 1904 in the *Chicago American.* It wasn't for kids, however; it was code for giving tips on horse races. "Mutt and Jeff" started the same way, as "M.A. Mutt," before dropping its racing line to become an all-around strip favorite.

The golden age for comics was the period 1907 to 1920, when scores of strips began appearing all across the country: "Krazy Kat" (1911), the first general comic strip intentionally aimed at adults, "Bringing Up Father" (1913), both "Popeye" and the family saga, "Gasoline Alley" (1919), and career girl "Winnie Winkle" (1920).

The 1920s and '30s saw the introduction of such durable strips as "Tarzan," "Flash Gordon," "Dick Tracy," and perhaps the most beloved comic strip of all time, "Blondie." "Blondie" eventually became a series of popular movies, and is still read in over 1,200 newspapers. "Dick Tracy" reaches about 50 million readers in 500 daily papers.

The first comic book magazine was published in 1933 as an advertising giveaway for Proctor and Gamble. It was called "Funnies on Parade," and reproduced popular comic strips from the newspapers. The first regularly published series of comic books was "Famous Funnies." It was similar in content to "Funnies on Parade," but you could pick it up at the newsstand every month for a dime. "Famous Funnies" lasted 20 years, and an early edition in mint condition could set a collector back more than $5,000 today.

Collectors also pay dearly for the first "Action Comics," which appeared in 1938, and contained the first characters not from the funny papers but created specifically for comic books. In 1939, "Action" introduced Superman—a character with super-human powers—and fundamentally changed the comics forever.

Besides the comics themselves, comic book character collectibles—everything from dolls, and wristwatches to pull toys and music boxes—are getting big bucks from collectors. The tradition goes back to the beginning of comics. The first comic character collectible appeared only two years after the first comic. In 1897, the Yellow Kid appeared as a handpainted plaster doll seated atop an Easter egg.

New York's mayor, Fiorello LaGuardia, endeared himself to the public by reading the funnies to kids on the radio so they wouldn't have to miss them during a newspaper strike. And Brian Walker, who draws the "Hi and Lois" strip, has called the comics, "the last bastion of American decency." But comic strips have not gone 100 years without controversy.

Mussolini banned all comics in Italy in the1930s. In the 1950s, a U.S. Senate panel led by Estes Kefauver investigated comics and found that they contributed significantly to juvenile delinquency. This forced the industry to censor itself by a code still in effect today.

In the 1960s, the comic strip "Pogo" (created in 1946) became the conscience of the anti-establishment, and "Peanuts" (created in 1950) was read for its poignant social satire. During the same era, "Steve Canyon" was repeatedly condemned as being racist and militaristic.

Recently, readers of the Sunday funnies were introduced to a sympathetic gay character. And "Doonesbury" and "Mallard Duck" still battle it out left and right on daily editorial pages across the nation.

But after a hundred years the comics are still thriving. Surprisingly, studies have shown that the more educated you are, the more likely you are to read the funny papers. The average age for readers of the Sunday comics is 30-to 39-years-old.

Comic strips were counted for dead when radio arrived. Then, the movies and TV were going to be their demise. These days, however, it's neither the movies nor TV that speaks to a third of the human race daily. It's still the comic strips.

The toons speak to the antiques market, too. Any item, whatever it is, will always be more collectible if it features a comic strip character.

PART VII
Stories About Collectibles

Time To Visit Our
Uncle Sam Again

Many of the great countries of the world have been bombed by their enemies—England, France, Germany, Italy, Japan—and many great cities—London, Munich, Dresden, Hiroshima—have seen their buildings and monuments razed to the ground and so many of their citizens lost in the rubble.

Now we are one of them.

September 11, 2001 was a sort of Confirmation, our Bar-Mitzvah by fire into the world's family of adult nations. And like many an adolescent, we find ourselves struggling to figure out just what we're supposed to do now.

Students of history and of antiques, the stuff of history, will know how important it is for us to visit the past right now. We will find inspiration there, and valuable lessons.

Recently, a friend and neighbor brought me a log and diary from the time during World War II when her home was used as a twenty-four hour-observation post, watching for any unusual activity along the Atlantic coast.

Just leafing through these pages, with their notes on codes and sirens and practice drills, I realized how civilians from Maine to Florida were involved in this sort of thing and how important the Homefront was to our victory in that war.

In the years since 9-11, Uncle Sam has made a reappearance around the country, especially in editorial cartoons.

The New York Daily News reproduced a copy of sheet music from the First World War featuring a giant Uncle Sam placing ships in the New York harbor. The song was "Wake Up America," and some of it's lyrics were:

"Are we ashamed of our history

In the peace that fighting brought?

Must we be laughed at, America,

While our swords turn weak with rust."

Maybe it's time to call on Uncle Sam again.

There was a time when Uncle Sam was everybody's favorite uncle. During the Depression he gave us jobs when there were no jobs, and helped us save for retirement. All he had to do was point at us and we joined his army, bought his war bonds and used his ration stamps, because we knew he had our best interests at heart.

His name was first heard during the War of 1812. The U.S. government contracted with a merchant in upstate New York, Samuel Wilson, to deliver provisions to the Army. When the goods arrived, stamped "U.S.," the grateful soldiers called them packages from their Uncle Sam.

Still, it would be a couple of decades before the figure of Uncle Sam would show up as a symbolic representation of the U.S. government. Instead, cartoonists and illustrators relied on two characters, Sam's predecessors: Brother Jonathan and Yankee Doodle.

Brother Jonathan goes way back to Revolutionary War times. He was supposed to be the younger brother of John Bull, the corpulent chap with a cane and top hat that cartoonists used to represent Great Britain.

Tall and lanky as Uncle Sam would be, Jonathan was sometimes illustrated with a top hat and pants with stars or stripes. He was often called "Yankee Jonathan," and when he was all dressed in stars and stripes, cartoonists called him "Yankee Doodle."

The term "Yankee" comes from the early Massachusetts Indians' name for the English colonists. A "doodler" is an old British term for a restless jack-of-all-trades, which is how the English viewed Americans. Perhaps our most famous doodler was Benjamin Franklin.

No one knows when Uncle Sam made his first appearance, but there is an editorial lithograph published by Henry R. Robinson in 1838 that depicts both Uncle Sam and Brother Jonathan.

The topic is Andrew Jackson's involvement in the collapse of the Bank of the United States, and it's clear that Uncle Sam represents the government and Jonathan represents the American people.

One artist, Frank H.T. Bellew, a *Harper's* illustrator and founder of *Vanity Fair*, used Uncle Sam so consistently (starting around 1852), that he is sometimes credited with being the man who made Sam so popular.

It was about this period that Uncle Sam grew his famous goatee. Some people in those times considered a man who shaved his face to be too vain. During the Lincoln-Douglas debates, Douglas remarked about the clean-shaven Lincoln: "How can anyone trust a fair-faced man."

The story is told that, when Lincoln was running for President, he received a note from a 12-year-old girl telling him that if he grew a beard he might have a better chance of getting elected. So Lincoln grew a beard, and so did Uncle Sam.

The most famous depiction of Uncle Sam, and the one that made him the exclusive symbol of the U.S. government, was the "I Want You" poster.

This image was the creation of James Montgomery Flagg, an illustrator for New York's *Leslie* magazine, and first appeared on the cover on July 6, 1916 with the caption "What are you doing for preparedness."

The face of Uncle Sam is Flagg's own. He dressed up and did a self-portrait pointing at a mirror.

When America went to war in 1917, the Army used Flagg's Uncle Sam as a recruiting poster with the caption underneath: "I Want You

For U.S. Army" and in smaller letters, "nearest recruiting station." The poster came back in 1941 to recruit for World War II.

The wide variety of objects featuring the image of Uncle Sam is a chronicle of a nation proudly in love with its own image. It's a feeling we could use again.

Of course, Uncle Sam's initials spell US. So, if every last one of US decided to go to the polls and vote every November, maybe we could fix Uncle Sam and make him into that likeable fellow we used to know. We owe it to the old guy.

After all, he's family.

The Dog Days

I wrote a poem once about the month of August. It was a pretty good poem and managed to get itself published, twice, and the second time in the *New York Times Sunday Magazine*, which is a great deal more than you can expect of most poems. I shouldn't burden you with it here, except to say that its point was to change or at least modify the ancient superstition that August was an evil month when malignant influences prevail—the "dog days."

The Greeks called them *hemenai kunoidos* and the Romans, *dies caniculares*.

The name comes from the heliacal (with the sun) rising of the Dog Stars, Sirius, the brightest of the fixed stars and the major star in the "Greater Dog" constellation, and Polycon, the major star in the constellation known as the "Lesser Dog."

August was considered a pernicious time because it can be so hot, humid and buggy. And even though we humans could do things to make ourselves more comfortable, dogs, being at the mercy of the elements, were more apt to run mad in the streets.

There is an ancient truth to this, and a lesson that we should turn our attention to our dogs at this time of year, help them do what they can't do for themselves. We can change their water bowls more often;

we can cool them off with a shower, bath, or an occasional damp cloth; we can brush them and try to keep the bugs to a minimum without scorching their skin with chemicals.

One year as the dog days began, I had to do a special favor for my own dog, Tabou. I had to have her put to sleep. She was a 12-year-old beautiful, all-black, German Shepherd. I had found her, or she had found me, when she was a very sick 8-month-old puppy abandoned on the streets of Brooklyn, New York. I had hoped she would be with me as long as my first dog, who lived for 17 years. But Tabou developed a degenerative sickness that her breed is genetically predisposed to. I wasn't prepared for how much I would miss her.

The statistics these days show that cats have overtaken dogs as the number one pet in America. This probably has to do with more apartment and condo living and certain modern lifestyles that demand more freedom and less responsibility. You don't have to walk a cat and you can leave food out that it will only eat when it is hungry.

Dogs need you. They need you so much that before long you start needing them. It's not only that they need you for food and basic care, but also for companionship and affection. And sometimes they demand these things when we are so wrapped up in our own lives that we are not in the mood for giving. That they make us give at these times is probably the most wonderful thing they do for us. But in an age when "interdependency" is considered a dirty word, dogs are bound to slip a bit in popularity.

Dog stories, I know, often can be mawkishly sentimental. There is *Lassie* and *Benji* and *Old Yeller*. But there's also Steinbeck's Travels with

Charlie, and Nick and Nora Charles' Asta, and my personal favorite, Pedee, the "Our Gang" dog. And 50,000 years before Hollywood made its first movie, men and women were drawing pictures of dogs on the walls of their caves.

Dogs have been domesticated since before recorded history. The idea might have started among a tribe once inhabiting what is now Denmark. Today's dogs are the descendants of the grey wolves that followed men around for the scraps we slobs left all over wherever we went. Before long we found if we fed them directly, we could use dogs for all sorts of things.

A dog can find things. Its sense of smell is so acute it can pick out a specific item you touched as long as 10 days ago from among hundreds of other things. Dogs can hear sounds 100 hundred yards away that we can't hear 10 feet away from us. And although dogs see only in shades of black and white, they can detect movement better than we can and, like cats, they possess an incredible night vision called "eye shine."

More importantly, dogs are loyal and loveable. Frederick the Great once said: "The more I see of men, the more I love my dogs." Of course, Frederick was a king and would obviously be more comfortable if men were more like dogs. It has been said, "Every man is Napoleon to his dog." But if you are among those who think that a dog is too dumb to be independent or to have its own personality, you never owned a dog.

"He cannot be a gentleman that loveth not a dog," is an old saying, probably coined by an Englishman. Of the more than 160 breeds of dogs in the world, 25 percent are of English origin. And, in 1735, the

English were the first to require dog licenses as a humane measure. The English and the Germans have especially celebrated the dog in art. Staffordshire pottery dogs have been popular since the 1700s, and dogs are frequently featured on German game dishes and other hunting-related items.

Dogs have been used as symbols of loyalty and fidelity in all cultures. The Chinese Foo dogs and Japanese lion dogs are imperial symbols, warning that only the loyal are welcome in the palace. All over the world, aristocrats, clergymen, saints and businessmen have had dogs featured in their portraits. Dogs are particularly prominent in wedding scenes; in fact, in early Europe, a portrait of a couple featuring a dog had the power of a documented wedding license.

But dogs and the month of August get a bad rap from this "dog days" tag. August is what all of nature has been working toward. It is a time when everything is at its ripest and richest. The next month, it is downhill and the cycle has to start again. But this is as good as it gets.

"… this, this for which

all has been longing so long

and from which all too soon declines

again, again to those cold days

when the only hope there is

is for these days to come again."

So there, I did manage to get in some lines from my poem. But every school child knows that August is really the last month of the year, and we should make the most of it. If these are the dog days, let's take a cue from the dogs: find a cool spot, lie down and enjoy it.

A few days after Tabou was gone, I went to the Ocean City Humane Society to see if there was a dog who wanted to come home with me and help fill the emptiness I felt. They all did, and I wanted them all. But I made friends especially with a 7-month-old puppy I thought was a Dalmatian, but when her spots began to show better, I discovered her to be part English Setter. I never really cared what breed she was. I made baby sounds at her like you sometimes do to a puppy, and her name turned out to be LouLou.

"There is no doubt," wrote the critic and playwright Robert Benchley, "that every healthy, normal boy should own a dog at sometime in his life, preferably between the ages of 45 and 50." I had just turned 46 when I got LouLou and we've enjoyed many a wonderful August together.

The Advertising Game

Since those working on Madison Avenue refer to themselves as being in the "advertising game," let's make a real game of it. Here are some questions to test your knowledge of famous advertising characters. The answers are below. It's okay to peek; no one will know.

1. What obnoxious advertising character made his first appearance in a commercial on *The Tonight Show* with Jack Paar in 1963 and was assured success when an amused Paar insisted, "Let's run that again"?

2. What "sorry" undersea character's voice was dubbed for 20 years by veteran *Fiddler on the Roof* actor, Herschel Bernardi?

3. What macho advertising star was given the first name, "Veritably" after a contest in 1962?

4. After disappearing in the 1960s and '70s, what bubbly character was brought back in a 1980 commercial to ski down a slope with Sammy Davis Jr., honoring that year's Winter Olympics?

5. What roly-poly character's trademark high-pitched giggle came from the same voice that growled and sneered as the villain, Boris Badenov, of Bullwinkle cartoon fame?

6. What magazine logo character made his first appearance as a write-in candidate for president in 1956?

7. What salty gentleman was actually the creation of a 14-year-old schoolboy who won a contest in 1916?

8. What advertising character became so popular in the 1940s and '50s she was featured in a Hollywood movie, sold war bonds, appeared on TV's *What's My Line*, and received several honorary university degrees?

9. You can tell these three characters apart by the hats they wear—a chef's hat, a stocking cap and a British military hat. Who are they?

10. What advertising character started out in 1902 as a bad boy in one of the first syndicated comic strips in America?

So, how did you do? These were tough questions, I know. Collecting advertising character memorabilia can still be fun and games, however, and it's getting more profitable.

Here are the answers to our quiz. Did you peek?

1. "How about a nice Hawaiian Punch?" asks Punchy. "Sure," says the gullible Oaf. Then, Wham! the oaf gets it right in the kisser. Jack Paar thought the debut commercial so funny, he ran it again. And Punchy continued roundhousing the poor Oaf for 30 years, including a stint in the '70s with Donny and Marie Osmond.

2. Actor Herschel Bernardi was the voice of Charlie the StarKist Tuna for 20 years, saying things like (about ballet), "It looks stupid, but if you do it on tiptoes it is interpretive dancing and reveals your good taste to all." Sorry, Charlie.

3. In 1958 Proctor & Gamble knocked Lestoil out of the number one spot in all-purpose household cleansers by introducing the big guy,

Mr. Clean. "Veritably" was his winning first name in a company contest held in 1962.

4. "Speedy" the Alka-Seltzer character appeared in 212 television commercials from 1953 to 1964. The method for making these animated commercials was such a trade secret that the techniques were kept in a bank vault near the Hollywood studio where they were made. He made the Sammy Davis commercial in 1980, after being shelved by the company for almost 20 years

5. The high-pitched voice of the Pillsbury Doughboy, Poppin' Fresh, was dubbed by Paul Frees, who also did Boris Badenov for the Bullwinkle cartoons. Poppin' made his first appearance in 1960, and has been shyly giggling ever since.

6. Alfred E. Neuman, the cover boy for *Mad* magazine, is actually a face that's been around since the turn of the century. No one knows who the creator was, and it's generally considered some sort of folk art that caught on, especially at college campuses. When he first appeared on *Mad's* cover in 1956, the editors named him Alfred Neuman, after the music conductor on the Henry Morgan radio show. They added the "E" for no particular reason.

7. Planters' Mr. Peanut was the prize-winning creation of a 14-year-old schoolboy in a 1916 company contest. Today he is one of the world's most recognizable advertising characters.

8. Since she first made her appearance in 1936, Elsie the Borden cow has been something of a national treasure. She outdrew the G.M. Futurama exhibit during the second year of the New York World's Fair in 1940, with her "Barn Colonial" decor. In the same year, she appeared in the RKO movie, *Little Men*. Hubby Elmer took over at

the Fair. Baby Beulah appeared the next year to complete the wholesome American family.

9. For Kellogg's Rice Crispies, Snap appeared first in 1932 wearing a chef's hat. By the end of the decade, he was joined by Crackle in a stocking cap and Pop in a British military cap. Known in Sweden as *Piff, Paff och Puff,* and in Germany as *Knisper, Knasper und Knusper,* they are the first and longest-running advertising characters to represent the Kellogg company.

10. Buster Brown and his dog, Tige, were the creations of Richard Outcault, and appeared for the first time in a New York *Herald* comic strip on May 4, 1902. Buster was a naughty boy, always getting into trouble. But the strips usually ended with Buster making a resolution to be better. The strip caught the eyes of executives of the Brown Shoe Co. but Outcault started his own ad agency, selling Buster as a trademark to over 40 companies. Only Brown Shoe and Buster Brown Apparel survived.

All Aboard For Christmas

There is a charming little village on the New Jersey Cape—maybe you've seen it—where the snow lies on the ground year-round, and Santa and his reindeer are always flying over the snow-capped roofs.

If you haven't seen this village yet, you'll have to look hard, because this little hamlet is just a very small part of the spectacular operating model railroad at Joe Jones' Flyertown Toy Train Museum on Route 9 in Clermont.

No, this is not just any old toy train set. This is a score of different train lines snaking through a whole microcosm of little villages, towns, suburbs, small cities, and a big city, complete with skyscrapers that Jones built himself.

Besides the buildings, there are cliffs and trees, tunnels, water towers, electric towers, and billboards. There are cars, trucks, barrel loaders, log loaders and cranes. Hundreds of people are working and playing everywhere—strolling the streets, shopping the stores, tending brakes, loading freight, waiting at lonely stations in the country, and packed on the commuter platforms of the cities.

"Holy Mackerel!" I gasped, as Jones flicked the switch bringing this huge little world to life. "That's just about everybody's first reaction," Jones said with a satisfied smile.

I defy anyone, in the face of all this, not to become a kid again. You'll find your eyes widening and your jaw going slack, as the outside world melts away and so do the years. I can't remember the last time I said "Holy Mackerel!" that way about anything.

Jones, who works for the Federal Aeronautics Administration, opened the Flyertown Museum in 1996. He received his first train set when he was a year old, and it's right up there among the crush of individual engines, cars and complete sets that cram the shelves along three of the four walls inside the museum.

"Collectors today usually line up between pre-and post-World War II trains," says Jones, who lists himself among the post-war S-gauge collectors. He is a member of the Train Collectors of America and the National Association of S-Gaugers.

Jones offers more than just a spectacular display at his museum. He is also a walking encyclopedia of model railroads. He conducts his tours personally, and if in the unlikely event that he can't answer your questions, he'll quickly tell you where to find the answers.

The train set has been a part of Christmas, circling around the Christmas tree, since the late 19th Century. Beginning in the 1860s, the cars were pulled or pushed along by hand or operated by windup clockworks. Then, in the 1890s, the first electric trains started to appear, but so few families had electricity, the manually operated kind were produced right on through the turn of the century.

In 1901, the Lionel company produced its first electric trains in what they called a standard gauge (2½-inches between the rails) until 1915, when they switched to their current O-gauge (1¼") with three rails.

American Flyer trains were produced for years, but the company really took off when it was purchased by A.C. Gilbert in 1937. They made smaller S-gauge (7/8") trains with two-rail tracks.

Both companies dominated the toy train market up through the 1950s. Now they are both produced by a privately owned company called Lionel Trains Inc. Marx and Ives also made model trains during this period. American Models and S. Helper are among today's most popular brands.

All aboard for Christmas! It's always just around the bend.

Duffers' Delights

The story is told of an old pastor who was golfing with his young cleric. Neither of the padres was doing too well on the course, and after a particularly poor drive, the pastor sighed, "Ah, my boy, we must give it up." "What, golf?" asked the cleric. "No," the pastor said emphatically, "the ministry!"

That a minister should abandon his flock to spend more time improving his golf game would probably not seem absurd to any dedicated duffer. Many golfers are equally religious in their fervor for the game. They'd rather be on the golf course than just about anywhere else.

The same zeal for golf is shared by collectors of golf memorabilia. They are constantly on the lookout for anything connected to the sport.

Golf tees are particularly collectible, both surface tees and inserted tees.

For centuries golfers had teed off a mound of wet sand constructed by a caddy. By the mid-19th Century, groundskeepers were providing boxes of sand, called tee boxes, at each teeing area, and the caddy was equipped with a little conical mold to form the tee.

Artificial tees appeared at the end of the 19th Century, but most golfers still used the sand tee, which didn't completely disappear until around 1920. The earliest artificial tees were surface tees that laid flat on the surface of the grass. They could be constructed of anything from paper to lead-weighted cast iron or heavy rubber.

"Reddy tee" (1920s) was the first of the conventional inserted tees. The old ones are rarely worth more than a few dollars today, unless they do something unusual like swivel. The most interesting thing about them is the names under which they were marketed: "Daintee," "Infini-tee," "Launching Pad," Strip-Tees," etc.

Not long ago, a gutta-percha golf ball, marked "ALLAN" for its maker, Allan Robertson, fetched a record $40,000.

The reason the ball was so expensive is because Robertson resisted making gutta percha balls, preferring the earlier feather balls. In fact, he became so enraged at the introduction of the so-called "gutty balls" in the late 1840s, that he bought up as many as he could and burned them. And when he found his longtime assistant, Tom Morris, playing golf with a gutty, he fired him.

There are supposedly fewer than 500 original feather balls in existence today, and prices run high, especially if they are signed balls. They are often confused with another feather-filled leather ball made for an English game called "Fives." True golf feather balls should have only one visible seam and should feel just about as hard as a modern golf ball.

There are many more solid gutta-percha balls in existence. They dominated the game until about 1900, when they were replaced with rubber-core gutty balls. Most factory-made gutty balls bring several hundred dollars. Hand-forged, signed and unusually designed guttys have been auctioned off in the thousands of dollars.

The modern golf ball was introduced in the 1920s. It has a rubber core, wrapped with thread and covered with a surface of dimpled balata, a rubber-like substance. Before the '20s, there was no standard golf ball size and weight. There was even such a thing as "floaters," large, lightweight balls that floated in water hazards so they could be easily recovered.

The process of standardizing golf balls began in the 1920s. By 1932, they were standardized in America as 1.62 ounces and 1.68 inches in diameter. The British used the smaller 1.62 inch until 1974, when they officially adopted the larger American size, as did the rest of the world in January, 1983.

Modern golf balls have to be quite special to be worth anything. Presidential golf balls in signed boxes have been issued (at taxpayer expense) as souvenirs since the times of Taft, Wilson and Harding, even by presidents like Reagan and Carter, who didn't play the game.

As golf balls changed, so did the clubs, irons and putters. Today's golf clubs would have chewed up the old feather balls.

Collectible clubs are dated by three categories: Antique (anything before 1930, but most often found today from 1910 to 1930), Wood Shafts, also called the Common Hickory (1925 to about 1940), and

Classic Clubs (1940s through the 1960s), especially those made for or endorsed by famous golf pros.

The prices in each of these categories vary widely, and many of the old golf clubs we find in attics and garages are of little value. But don't take any chances. Do a bit of research before you throw anything out or put it out for a couple of dollars at a yard sale.

Among the most sought-after golf clubs today are the cleek-marked clubs and the patent irons.

Before the 1880s golf irons were made by blacksmiths. After the 1920s, they were factory made. The time in between (1880-1920s) golf irons were made by cleek makers, blacksmiths who turned exclusively to making golf irons. About 90 percent of these craftsmen stamped their work with what are known as cleek marks. Today, some of these "cleek marks" can boost an iron's value.

Patent clubs, both woods and irons, are the most interesting of the golf club collectibles. Patent clubs were developed and patented by inventors who promised to correct your problems and improve your game. These clubs squiggle, scoop, spoon or rake. Some have holes under them and/or through them, center shafts or double shafts, grooved heads, mesh heads or dimpled heads. These funny-looking contraptions are a testament to how frustrated golfers can become and how gullible they can be in search of a better game.

The Story Of Raggedy Ann

The Raggedy Ann doll was patented by Johnny Gruelle on September 7, 1915. Gruelle, who was born on Christmas Day, 1889, was a cartoonist, illustrator and writer of children's stories. The real life story behind that patent, however, is what makes Raggedy Ann and her friends so special.

One day Gruelle's young daughter, Marcella, found an old handmade rag doll in their Connecticut attic. Gruelle fixed it up, painted on a smiling face and attached a little cutout cardboard heart.

He called the doll Raggedy Ann from two poems by James Whitcomb Riley, "The Raggedy Man" and "Orphan Annie," and it became Marcella's favorite doll.

But Marcella died at the age of fourteen after a long illness. The devastated Gruelle dealt with his grief by writing down the stories he had made up for her over the years about Raggedy and her friends.

Gruelle's publisher, P. F. Vollard, asked to publish the stories and suggested that Gruelle make up some dolls to promote them. Before long, Gruelle had more orders for dolls than he could handle.

In 1918 Vollard got a manufacturer to take over production. Raggedy's cardboard heart disappeared in favor of one that was painted on, and there were other design changes but the trademark smile remained the same.

Over the years the Raggedy Ann doll acquired some friends from the stories Gruelle had made up: Raggedy Andy, Beloved Belinda (a black doll), Percy the Policeman, Uncle Clem, Little Brown Bear and Eddie Elephant.

In 1935 Raggedy was produced by Molly Goldman's company, Molly-es Doll Outfitters, with a printed rather than painted face. The Exposition Doll & Toy Company also made Rageddies in the '30s, but only for a brief time, making their dolls among the rarest.

Georgene Novelties, Inc. produced Raggedy Ann with a black outline around the traditional triangular nose.

The Knickerbocker Toy Co. gave Raggedy Ann a couple of more friends: The Camel with the Wrinkled Knees and Raggedy Arthur.

Hasbro and Applause also made Raggedies, with Hasbro producing a special Christmas Raggedy in 1988. The license for the Raggedies now belongs to McMillan, Inc.

Mammies, Sambos And Pickaninnies

It's hard to fathom that less than 60 years ago the U.S. military was still racially segregated and that integrating the armed forces was heavily resisted by those who insisted that it would lead to a breakdown in discipline and that it would be unthinkable to ask white soldiers to live, work and fight alongside blacks.

It's equally difficult to realize that less than 50 years ago, African-American citizens in many parts of this their country were forced to sit in the back of buses, use separate water fountains and restrooms, eat at separate restaurants, stay at separate hotels and send their children to separate schools.

In those dark days of institutional racism, however, there was another kind of racism pervading the country that may have been more devastating because those who practiced it felt it was benign.

This was the stereotyping of African-Americans as cute and cuddly caricatures: Mammy, Aunt Jemima, the coon, the golliwog, Sambo, Topsy Turvy, Honey Pie and the pickaninny, among others.

These caricatures were an intricate part of American culture for decades. From the mid-19th Century through the middle of the 20th Century, they can be found quite matter-of-factly in advertising art, sheet music, souvenirs, toys, postcards, posters, prints and household items, especially those for the kitchen or the bar.

On the antiques market they are collectively called "Black Americana." Collector Whoopie Goldberg has called them "Negrobilia."

They are still cute, colorful, sometimes warm, and even very funny. It would be hypocritical to say otherwise, as long as we are able to face up to the unfortunate attitudes they represent. That's a confusing bunch of emotions to juggle, isn't it? Sort of like trying to be "politically correct." It's hard, and lots of people really don't like that term.

But if Black Americana teaches us anything, it's that sometimes being politically correct is just the correct way to be. In America, that means understanding, once and for all, that there can never be any second-class citizens in a country that has dedicated itself to the idea that all men are created equal.

The best antiques are those that truly evoke their times, and those times are not always what we would like them to have been. Sure, there is an innocence about the era of Black Americana, but we've grown up a bit since then. Haven't we?

A Bow To Royalty
Collectibles

Why do people collect British royalty commemoratives? Is it a class thing?

Maybe for some people, but I collected royalty commemoratives for a while, and it never was a class thing for me. I have sold off several pieces of my collection over the years, but I still have a few pieces left. They are prominently displayed on a ledge above a door in my office.

I swear it's only a coincidence that the door leads to the bathroom (throne room?).

In her annual message to the British Parliament, Queen Elizabeth II once referred to her recent family problems as causing her an *"annus horribilis"* (a dreadful year). No doubt it did.

Charles and Di had divorced, both admitting to carrying on adulterous affairs. Fergy and Andrew had divorced. She's the "Duchess of Pork," according to the tabloids. So she was cut off, banished to America to become a ... well, to sell herself as a spokesperson for a diet regimen.

Is there anything more delicious than a scandal at a tea party?

For those who are really scandalized by the behavior of the royals, I can only quote Joan Rivers: "Ah, grow up."

Considering the bloody and lecherous history of monarchs everywhere, and the British kind in particular, the petty peccadillos of the Windsor kids pale in comparison.

Isn't the older generation supposed to be scandalized by the younger generation?

At least in this case it could be the other way around. Only people who don't know history can insist that folks were always better in the good old days.

Even in the fairy tales, royal position has never been an assurance of saintly behavior. Consider the evil queen in Snow White. And what about Alice's encounter with that awful Queen of Hearts, always shouting: "Off with her head!"?

Ironically, while it might have been a dreadful year for the royals, collectors of British royalty commemoratives have been enjoying an annus mirabilis (a marvelous year). There is nothing like a touch of scandal to boost celebrity. And on today's collectibles market, it seems, celebrity sells.

The Royals are stars, and people collect things having to do with all sorts of stars (Elvis, Marilyn, James Dean, JFK), despite what some people—those without sin or not in glass houses—might consider the star's shortcomings.

We are fascinated by people who seem to have it all—wealth, fame, looks, power. Writers from William Shakespeare to Jackie Collins have exploited that fascination. What we usually learn is that "having it all" is always far less than having what we really need.

I started collecting British royalty commemoratives as part of a broader collection of heads and faces, a popular field these days, judging by the ads and articles in the current trade publications. Most commemoratives feature a portrait or profile of the honored royal on the occasion of his or her birth, christening, coronation, wedding, anniversary, jubilee (years on the throne), or death.

Of course, some of the older commemoratives could give me that time-travel sensation that antique-lovers get when an object strongly evokes an era or the events of history. That's one thing about the royals: everything they do becomes history.

A commemorative of Edward VIII, for instance, is all the more socially and historically poignant, because of the drama (and scandal) surrounding his abdication in favor of a marriage to that Mrs. Simpson, a divorced commoner!

I also couldn't help noticing the potential decorative value of royal commemoratives. They are particularly striking set among the traditional English mahogany styles like Chippendale, Hepplewhite and Sheraton. And they are graceful and appropriate in the Victorian room, a style named for the mother of all today's royals.

Many commemorative pieces will stand on their own in any decor. That's because they are simply beautiful, fine examples from some of the most important names in the decorative arts: Wedgwood, Royal Doulton, Royal Crown Derby, Royal Worcester, and others.

Even some of the lesser-known firms seem to put out their best work when creating a royalty piece. Be especially on the lookout for limited edition pieces.

A well-chosen collection of British royalty commemoratives may or may not be a class thing, a star thing, a history thing or a decorative thing. But they are an "in" thing now, and that may be a smart thing.

Oyster Plates 'R' Always In Season

"Let us royster with the oyster—in the shorter days and moister,

That are brought by brown September, with its roguish final R;

For breakfast or for supper, on the shell or upper,

Of dishes he's the daisy, and of shell-fish he's the star."

This little ditty was published in the *Detroit Free Press* on October 12, 1889, right in the middle of America, just as oysters were becoming a treasured treat across the country.

It is because oysters were so treasured that the special and beautiful items made to serve and eat them have become such treasures in today's antique shops.

Actually, oysters can and always could be eaten any time of the year, not just during months with "R's" in them. The tradition of avoiding oysters from May through August evolved from a French law passed in 1750, which made it illegal to harvest oysters during those months.

The French were trying to protect their supply of the precious *huîtres* from a public that had begun to devour them at an alarming rate. It was not unheard of, for instance, for some gentlemen of the era to slurp down 100 oysters at a single sitting, often at breakfast.

Oyster plates, fancy dishes for serving the delectable bivalves, were produced primarily to serve canned oysters, developed in the 1880s. The plates continued to be produced in quantity up through the 1920s until the fad for oysters faded with the arrival of the great Depression.

Oyster plates feature molded oyster or clam-shaped wells, and usually have a center well for oyster sauce. Some also have additional small wells for lemon wedges.

Contrary to some rumors, the price of a dish does not increase with the number of wells. Most oyster dishes have four to seven wells, but there are also single-well oyster plates ("shooters"), and triple wells in unusual shapes that command high prices for their rarity.

Collecting oyster plates has become such a rage these days that you won't find many under $100. Oyster plates, in general, are real rarities. That's why collectors love them.

But as rare as they are, there is an incredible variety for collectors to choose from, including different shapes, designs, colors materials and manufacturers

Porcelain oyster plates from Limoges, France, are especially desirable. When they are marked, you will most often see the finest factories represented: Haviland & Co., Charles Field Haviland, Theodore Haviland, T&V (Tressemann & Vogt), CA (Ahrenfeldt), JP (Jean Pouyat), and others. If they are marked "France," they were made after 1891.

Minton seems to have made the most English oyster plates, and some of them are spectacular. But also look for names like Wedgwood, Doulton, George Jones, Worcester and Holdcroft.

Faience and majolica are two terms for earthenware that has been coated with a heavy tin glaze. The term "majolica" is usually reserved for very colorful pieces with decorations in relief.

These are among the most sought-after oyster dishes today. Some marks to look for include Quimper and Sarreguemines from France, and Griffin, Smith and Hill, Etruscan and Phoenix Pottery from the U. S.

Lucky collectors will find Dresden and Meissen porcelain oyster plates from Germany. The question is: will they want to pay the high prices? Other German companies, like Weimar, Carl Tielsch, etc., might be more affordable. Plates marked "Victoria" and "Carlsbad" are among the best from Austria.

Other ceramic oyster plates include those exclusively made for restaurants, railroads and steamship lines, and Satsuma pottery from Japan. But oyster plates were not only produced in pottery and porcelain. Collectors looking to broaden their collections will try to find the finest Bohemian art glass from Ludwig Moser, as well as plates in pewter and the very rare silver plates.

There are plenty of oyster plate "go-withs" attracting collectors today. Among the most popular are the colorful labels on the old oyster cans. Collectors also look for oyster forks, oyster serving spoons, tureens and serving plates.

With all this talk about rarity, variety and value, we might be missing the point about why people collect oyster plates. It's basically because they are beautiful. Oysters were considered a delicacy, second only to caviar, and the dishes they were served in were expected to do them justice—and they certainly do.

Oyster facts: The word oyster comes from the Greek *osteron*. The Greeks regularly consumed the mollusks, and used the shells as ballots by scratching the name of their candidate inside.

The French king, Louis XI, really believed oysters were brain food. He insisted that the professors at the Sorbonne eat oysters at least once a year, "lest their scholarship become deficient."

"He was a bold man that ate the first oyster" is a line from the English satirist Jonathan Swift (1667-1745), who wrote "Gulliver's Travels." We don't know who that first man was, but studies indicate that men were eating oysters 8,000 years ago.

Since you don't share a single oyster, the phrase, "The world is my oyster," means that everything you see is yours. The line comes from Shakespeare's "Merry Wives of Windsor," when Pistol says in Act II: "Why the World's mine Oyster Which I with sword will open."

In ancient Rome, the author of one of the world's earliest known cookbooks, Apicus, committed suicide when he could no longer afford the great expense of importing oysters from Britain to serve his guests.

Oyster plates might be a costly indulgence these days, but collectors now have saner ways of coping with the expense. Poor Apicus, after all, didn't have a Master Card.

It's Always Teatime For Collectors

"Tea is adored by monks and poets.

Prepared in white jade dishes couched in softest red silk,

The topaz-hued leaves are yours very quickly

Ready to accompany you to enjoy bright moon of night

And to greet the rosy clouds of early dawn.

Never in ancient or modern times

Has anyone ever tired of taking it.

Never can it be praised too much

In the presence of those who are drinking it."

—Ancient Chinese poem

With the possible exception of the dry martini, few beverages have had such a fuss made about them as tea.

Like the martini, tea is not just served, but performed with great ceremony, involving all the necessary accouterments of a proper ritual.

Tea became a way of life for the English very early in the Victorian era (1837-1901).

It all began one afternoon in 1840, when Anna, the seventh Duchess of Bedford, experienced what she described as a "sinking feeling." To raise her spirits, she ordered up some tea and cakes. Before long she had made a habit of punctuating her afternoons this way, eventually inviting her friends to join her.

The duchess really did have a jolly good idea. At that time in England there were only two meals a day. An enormous breakfast, including meat, fish, eggs, bread and biscuits was supposed to hold you over until dinner in the evening.

So, teatime was good idea, but why make such a to-do about it?

Part of the reason is because making a to-do was something Victorians loved to do, especially at mealtime. There were special plates and utensils for just about every food on the table and a special etiquette for serving and for eating it. Also, with tea time, the English public were following the example of a duchess, and we all know what a to-do a duchess can do when she has a mind to.

But the ritualizing of teatime started long before the Duchess of Bedford, around 400 B.C., with the Buddhist monks who were the sole consumers of tea until it became a popular drink in the Orient around 1200 A.D.

The monks drank tea to help them stay awake for long hours of prayer. They developed a ceremony around the preparation, serving and drinking of the tea. Versions of this ceremony were adopted as the "way of tea" by the Chinese (Ch'a Ching) and the Japanese (Cha Do).

By using special accessories and requiring a special etiquette, teatime for the Orientals, and eventually the English, became a time when you could fully abandon the outside world and concentrate on something else, so you might emerge truly refreshed and energized.

For the English, tea should steep just five minutes. There are tea timers for this, but the traditional measure is the length of time it takes to recite the 51st Psalm, a tract asking the Lord to cleanse and renew the soul.

English "high tea" sounds regal and formidable, but it really just refers to the table on which tea is served. High tea is served at the dining room table; low tea is served in the parlor at a lower tea table.

Teatimes can be formal or informal. Formal tea is served from a silver tea set with linen napkins. At informal teas, a pottery or porcelain tea service is used, and paper napkins are acceptable.

It's always teatime for collectors, who are forever grabbing up interesting tea accessories at the antique shops.

Teapots top the list. It's hard to find English pots from the late 18th and early 19th Centuries, but there are still some interesting Victorian pots from the big Staffordshire companies like Wedgwood, Spode, Worcester, Derby, etc.

Popular English pots from the 20th Century include Sadler and Gibbon, as well as all the chintz pattern makers like Royal Winton. In 1948 Hall China was the largest teapot maker in the world, and they are the top choice among American teapots.

Other neat tea items include: tea strainers, infusers and immersers, lemon dishes and lemon forks, cups and saucers, spill bowls, scone or biscuit plates, tea bag drops, trivets, hot pads, tongs and caddies.

Also available in antique shops are tea towels and napkins, tea tables and samovars (tea urns).

Should you be invited to a tea, high or low, remember these little rules of etiquette: Stir your tea in a clockwise manner, noiselessly. When drinking tea, your saucer should never be more than twelve inches from your cup and always look into your cup, never over your cup. Swallow food before drinking and swallow tea before eating. Never, under any circumstances, discuss the food. Eat it or decline it, but don't ask what it is, how it was made, or even compliment it.

Then there is the question of putting one's pinkie in the air. Apparently this tradition comes from the days before utensils, when everyone ate with their hands. Common folk used all five fingers to dig in, but aristocrats were instructed to use only three. Keeping one's pinkie in the air was a symbol that one had been bred well.

So, go ahead, do it; keep that pinkie high. It's actually kind of cute.

Hot Chocolate Days On The Antiques Market

Hot chocolate can warm us up on chilly winter days, but chocolate-related items are hot all year-round in antique shops.

Europeans didn't know a thing about chocolate until Christopher Columbus brought a few cocoa beans back to Ferdinand and Isabella. Unfortunately, no one knew what to do with them.

Soon after, however, the Spanish explorer, Hernando Cortés, learned the secret, when he and his men were asked to join the Aztec Emperor, Montezuma, in a goblet of "chocolatl," the Aztec word for "warm drink."

Montezuma told them it was a "divine drink which builds up resistance and fights fatigue. A cup of this precious liquid permits a man to walk a whole day without food."

Montezuma could have walked a whole lot more than that on his 50-cup-a-day habit. But he wasn't far off about the health benefits of chocolate—benefits we are only just realizing today.

Who would've thunk it. Chocolate is the highest natural source of magnesium, as well as a load of other vitamins and minerals that are beneficial against hypertension, cardiovascular disease and even the symptoms of PMS. It's the dark chocolate that's best for you.

It was Cortés' idea to add sugarcane to the bitter drink he shared with Montezuma, and for nearly 100 years the Spanish made a hefty profit selling chocolate throughout Europe. They kept the formula secret by producing it behind the cloistered walls of monasteries.

There were major advances in chocolate making during the 19th Century, beginning with the invention of a cocoa press in 1828.

The English invented solid "eating chocolate" in 1847, and Prince Albert introduced it to the world at the Crystal Palace Exposition in London in 1851. That's when Americans got their first taste of chocolate candy.

By the time the Swiss invented milk chocolate in 1876, chocolate had become something of a rage in Europe and America. That's when we begin to see an explosion in the production of the chocolate-related items that have made today's antique lovers into such chocoholics.

The leading chocolate collectible is the fancy porcelain chocolate set—a tall pot with a short spout high up under the lid accompanied by matching cups and saucers. Chocolate cups are just slightly taller than demitasse cups.

Finding a complete chocolate set is a rare treat, so some folks collect just the pots, and others just the cups and saucers. The key to great value, however, is in the richness of the decoration. The more ornate, the more gold, the more valuable the piece.

The finest chocolate sets were produced in Limoges by Haviland and other companies in that city, in Germany by the Schlegelmilch family (especially those marked RS Prussia), and those made in Japan and marked "Nippon" (1891-1921).

You can also find beautiful pieces marked by other German and Austrian companies, Japanese Noritake, and a few English companies like Royal Doulton.

Also popularly collectible are the chocolate candy molds, most of which were made by German companies, like Reiche and Gesetzl, from the turn of the century through the mid-1930s. These molds were made of nickle-plated tin or copper to produce chocolate figures mostly for holidays like Christmas, Easter, Valentine's Day and Halloween.

Also look for bonbon tongs (small sugar tongs), chocolate spoons (round bowl espresso spoons), silver bonbon trays and confection spoons.

Smoking Collectibles Are Really Hot Stuff

Mark Twain once wrote, "Nothing needs reforming like other people's habits."

He was, of course, satirizing that impulse many Americans have shared since the days of the Puritans to foist their personal views on their neighbors.

Nathaniel Hawthorne wrote scathingly of this phenomenon in stories like "The Maypole of Merry Mount," and it was another American author, perhaps Alexander Wolcot, who defined Puritanism as: "The sneaking suspicion that somebody somewhere is having a good time."

You would think that the disastrous failure of Prohibition would have cured folks of the crusading impulse, but in fact it has never been stronger, especially among today's antismoking forces.

Their zealotry, however, may have produced some unforeseen results. As the popularity of smoking declines, the value of old smoking items is increasing.

It's hard to believe that as little as fifty years or so ago smoking was considered chic and, yes, even good for you.

It wasn't uncommon to see cigarette ads in magazines featuring top athletes testifying about how smoking actually improved their game.

Smoking accessories were made of fine materials and exquisitely designed from such top companies as Wedgwood, Tiffany and Royal Crown Derby. No dinner table was set without a cigarette urn at each end of the table and an individual ashtray at each place setting.

At a friends house for dinner one recent evening, smokers were provided with an old coffee can and pointed toward the outdoor deck. It was raining.

Whatever your attitude about smoking, however, there is no disagreement among collectors that smoking-related paraphernalia are getting lots of attention on the antiques market.

Those huge, colorful glass ashtrays from Murano Italy that used to grace the cocktail tables of the 1950s have already become quite collectible.

Beautifully carved pipes—wood, ivory or meerschaum—are fine examples of skilled craftsmanship and are easy to display in old pipe racks. "Meerschaum," by the way, is the German word for sea foam. Named for its bright white color, it is actually a mineral found in the earth. Not all wood pipes are briar. Pipes were also carved out of walnut, boxwood and other woods. Truly fine pipes often had stems of real amber.

Humidors and tobacco jars are also collectible. The humidor will have a place inside the lid to insert a humidifying element, such as a damp sponge. These jars are especially sought after if they are figures of animals or people.

Old cigarette cases, cigarette holders and lighters, for men or women, were meant to be as stylish as jewelry, and the best ones really look it. Lovely cigarette urns and clever dispensers were just the thing for chic cocktail parties.

Other smoking items being collected include: tobacco-related advertising art and premiums, cigar cutters, smoking tables and stands, cigar boxes and tins, and even candy cigarette packs.

Tobacco trivia: The word "tobacco" comes from the Native American word for the calumet or long peace pipe. Settlers just misunderstood what they were being offered.

The word for the narcotic in tobacco, nicotine, comes from Jean Nicot, the French ambassador to Portugal. He sent some tobacco to Catherine de Medici, who claimed it cured her headaches. She was so happy, she officially proclaimed that the new plant be called "Nicotiana."

Sir Walter Raleigh, who made tobacco smoking fashionable in London, also started another tradition. It is reported that just before he was beheaded, he took a puff from his pipe, thus initiating the rite of the final smoke before execution.

If you think the Surgeon General's warnings about smoking are harsh, just listen to what England's James I proclaimed way back in 1600:

Smoking tobacco, the king said, was "a custom loathsome to the eye, hateful to the nose, harmful to the brain, dangerous to the lungs, and the black stinking fumes thereof nearest resemble the horrible Stygian smoke of the pit that is bottomless."

Do you think we could fit all that on a pack of Marlboros?

The Taste Of Success

Millions of people each year, as they have for centuries, toast the new year with a glass of champagne, that sparkling wine which has for so long been associated with good luck, prosperity and class.

For those who may frown on beginning the new year by indulging in what they perceive to be a bad habit, let us turn to Psalm 104, which thanks the Lord for "wine to gladden the heart of man" and for "water … so the jackasses may quench their thirst."

Champagne is doubly blessed, however, having been invented in the 1600s by a Benedictine monk, Dom Pierre Perignon, whose name now graces one of the most expensive brands of this pricey potable.

That is as it should be. After all, it is Perignon's process—complicated, time-consuming and labor-intensive—that is the primary reason why champagne is such a budget-buster.

The grapes for making true champagne must come for the area that was, in the *ancien régime*, the Province of Champagne, now the Departements of Marne, Aube and Aisne.

Only three wines from this region may be used: the black grapes Pinot and Meuniere, and the white Chardonnay. Sparkling wine made only with white grape is called "blanc de blanc"; pink champagne in made by adding a splash of red wine.

A simplified version of the process for making champagne goes like this: One of the area's wines is brought to initial fermentation in a cask. Then, the other permitted wines are blended in for taste. This is where the true artistry of creating champagne comes into play.

If the blended wines are all from the same year, the champagne can be labeled "vintage." The blend is then bottled for a second fermentation. During this process, the bottles are regularly tilted at various different angles until they are completely upside down.

The bottles remain upside down for weeks, until all the sediment has gathered at the cork. They are then uncorked, and the sediment is "blown off." A syrup of sugar and old champagne is added to induce a third fermentation. The bottles are finally recorked and wired shut. Champagne will continue to age in its bottle.

The preferred glass among today's champagne drinkers is the stately, tall and slender "flute," but you won't find too many of these in antique shops. That's because in previous decades, the elegant saucer was the stem glass of choice.

The rationale for the flute is that it not only holds more, but it contains the bubbles, keeping the costly concoction fresher in the glass.

The saucer-sippers, on the other hand, found extra pleasure in the escaping bubbles tickling their noses. Also, they assumed, there should only be a few sips in a champagne glass, the rest should be staying cold in the ice bucket.

All agree that champagne should be served icy cold. One passionate aficionado, Charles Baker, in his book "The Gentleman's Companion" (Crown, 1946) put it this way: "Warm champagne is a fetid thing, of brassy taste, astringent to the throat, an insult to the nostrils."

Everything else about champagne is much less dictatorial. It is okay, for instance, to serve champagne anytime during a meal and even throughout a meal. Champagne is considered a compliment to seafood, yet of bold enough character to stand up to meats.

Most agree that *brut*, or dry champagne, is best, but sweet champagnes—*sec, demi-sec* and *doux*—are better with desserts.

At most cocktail lounges today a Champagne Cocktail is simply champagne served by the glass.

The classic Champagne cocktail, however, is made by placing a sugar cube drenched with bitters (orange or Angostura) at the bottom of the glass, pouring a shot of cognac on top of that, then filling the glass with champagne. Garnish is usually a thin spiral of orange or lime peel.

Aside from New Year's Eve, we usually break out the champagne to celebrate a success or special occasion. I have always kept at least one bottle in my refrigerator at all times. It helps maintain an air of optimism, the feeling that sometime, hopefully soon, something wonderful will happen worthy of uncorking it.

You might say we enjoy this most special of wines at New Year's to congratulate ourselves for getting through another year. I think it's because we want to start the new year with the taste of success in our mouths.

Conversation Pieces

◆

A Christmas Story

Once upon a time, a not very long time ago, there were two antique dealers named Gus and Arnie, who each ran a shop out of his home along a two-mile cluster of about a dozen antique shops nestled in the New England countryside.

They were roughly the same age (mid-60s), and both single men—Gus was a bachelor and Arnie a widower—with no close family to speak of.

Despite their similarities, and although they worked many years in the same business in the same area, they were not as friendly with one another as you might expect of two people with otherwise so much in common.

Ironically, it was another similarity that kept them apart: they were both confirmed loners—misanthropes, you might say.

While they thought of themselves as just contentedly independent guys, it was the consensus of their neighbors that they were well on their way to becoming a couple of grumpy old men.

Of course, in the course of doing business, they couldn't totally avoid each other.

On those occasions when their paths did cross—auctions, shows, estate sales—they were polite enough to acknowledge one another with a nod or even a few words, but since they prided themselves on being men of few words, they never had any real conversations.

This was the case even when they visited each other's shop, which all good antique dealers have to do from time to time.

At those times, even when they found themselves alone, the talk never went beyond: "Hi, how are you?" … "Fine." … "How's business?" … "You know how it is—up and down."

Since many of these visits would occur in the late fall, when there was finally some time after the tourist crowds left, Gus and Arnie might also exchange a couple of words about the cold weather, as New Englanders often do.

It was on just such a cold New England day, with an early December's first dusting of snow on the bare branches of the white birch trees and on the tips of the evergreens, that Arnie showed up for a perfunctory view of what Gus had for sale in his shop.

Now, their shops were a bit different from each other, so while they might buy a little something from one another from time to time, these visits were mostly just to check on one another's inventory and prices.

On this particular visit, however, Arnie found Gus filling a large table with an extensive array of Christmas ornaments, which he was taking from several boxes arranged on the floor around him.

Arnie noticed a pig in a Santa suit, coming out of a chimney, a turtle with a Christmas tree on its back, a snake with a clown's head, an angel poling a gondola, a trolley car suspended from a dirigible.

As usual, the two men nodded their hellos and Gus, without looking up from his task, mumbled something about the snow. Arnie, of course, mumbled back a New England "yeah." But he couldn't take his eyes off the dazzling ornaments on the display table.

There were all manner of glass fruits and vegetables—pears, cucumbers, corn, lemons, carrots, strawberries and bananas—very few in anything close to their natural colors.

And there were birds, too, realistic and fanciful, enough to fill a whole tree. There were Santas and angels doing all sorts of things in cars, on motorcycles, in balloons and fire trucks.

Arnie suddenly couldn't contain himself and blurted out, "Get lucky at auction, did you?" Gus answered, "Nope," then despite himself added, "Actually they're mine," then he found himself adding still further—as he pulled out a pink and white beet painted with a Chinaman's face—"Family stuff; came down to me; last in the line, I guess."

They were both quiet for a while, as Gus pulled out an assortment of musical instruments, and fish and dogs and giraffes and insects and flowers and gingerbread men and snowmen and horses.

"Fascinating stuff. Must have been a interesting family," said Arnie.

Gus thought a bit as he pulled out a chicken wearing reindeer horns. Then he looked up right into Arnie's eyes and said, "You don't know the half of it."

Now, those of you who know the way Christmas stories work won't have to be reminded how something of a miracle took place here; how these two fellows, who rarely had a thing to say to each other, suddenly started gabbing and laughing and exchanging stories about their respective families and pasts.

You won't need for me to tack on a good old TV ending—about how Arnie and Gus became fast friends, and how Gus never sold the ornaments, and how magnificently decorated trees started showing up at children's wards and nursing homes, and how some special and deserving people in town, different ones each year, would receive Christmas ornaments delivered to their door with no return address.

There are folks, like some of Gus and Arnie's neighbors, and maybe even some of you, who might question how a simple conversation over some Christmas ornaments could make fast friends out of virtual strangers.

But Christmas is a very strange and magical time of year, if you hadn't noticed, when otherwise perfectly normal folks drag trees into their homes, and set them up right there in their living rooms.

Then, all these, well, *odd things* start appearing—bulldogs in top hats and smiling parsnips and monkeys with violins and sea horses in pine trees, rich guys on camels, and a God-Child born where animals eat.

Talk about your conversation pieces.

A Chronology For Antiquers

Valuable 18th Century Dates:

1643–1715	Louis XIV (Baroque)
1708	First European Porcelain—J. Boettger, Dresden Germany
1710	First European porcelain factory opens in Meissen, a Dresden suburb
1715–1774	Louis XV (Rococo)
1737 (ca.)	Caspar Wistar, a German immigrant, open the first commercially successful glass company in the Western Hemisphere in Upper Alloways (Salem County), New Jersey
1742	Thomas Boulsover, an English mechanic, develops silver plate on copper in the city of Sheffield
1776–1781	American Revolution
1774	Thomas Chippendale, "The Gentleman and Cabinet Maker's Guide"
1774–1792	Louis XVI (Neo-Classical)
1780–1820	Height of Sheffield plate production
1788	George Hepplewhite, "Cabinet-Maker and Upholsterer's Guide"
1789–1794	French Revolution
1791	Thomas Sheraton, "The Cabinet-Maker and Upholsterer's Drawing Book"

| 1790–c.1810 | American Federal style |
| 1794–1799 | French Directoire period |

Important 19th Century Dates:

1804–1814	Napoleon rules as "Emperor of the French"
1804–c.1830	French Empire style
1810	Josiah Spode introduces the "True Willow" pattern in Staffordshire
1810–c.1840	First American Empire (Duncan Phyfe) style
1812–1814	War of 1812
1815	Printed sampler patterns produced in Berlin (widespread in U.S. by 1830)
1815–c.1858	"Biedermeier" style (Austria/Germany)
1815–1830	Louis XVIII, France
1820	Deming Jarvis opens the Boston and Sandwich Glass Co., Sandwich (Cape Cod), Massachusetts.
1820	"German" silver developed, plating over white metal
1820	Gaslight widely available in homes
1822	First "fixed image" photo (pewter plate), J. Niepce, French
1824	"Les Roses," Pierre Joseph Redoute
1829	Photo iodized on silver, J. M. Daguerre (Daguerrotypes)
1830	Josiah Wedgwood II creates "Flow Blue" pottery
1830–1838	Charles Philippe Charles X
1837–1901	Victorian Age
1838	Electroplating of silver (Elkington)

1840	Anna, the seventh Duchess of Bedford initiates afternoon tea in England
1842	David Haviland, an American, opens a china-decorating studio in Limoges, France
1843	First Christmas card (Cole-Horsley), England
1848	Franz Josef ascends the throne of Austria
1850s	Cup plates discontinued in dinner and tea services
1850s–c.1890	Second American Empire (Pillar and Scroll) style
1851	Crystal Palace Exposition, London
1852–1870	Napoleon III, Second French Empire
1854	Treaty of Kanagawa (March 31), Commodore Perry opens Japan to the West
1861–1865	American Civil War
1865	David Haviland opens a china manufacturing plant in Limoges, France
1867–1916	Austro-Hungarian Empire
1868	Charles Locke Eastlake publishes "Hints on Household Taste"
1868	Celluloid plastic developed by John Wesley Hyatt
1869	Suez Canal opens
1870	Curved cutting wheel invented for cutting glass
1872	Eastlake's American edition published
1872	Montgomery Ward issues first catalogue
1874	Emile Galle opens a studio in Nancy, France
1875–c.1930	Arts and Crafts Movement
1876	American Centennial Exhibition in Philadelphia
1876–1916	American Brilliant Cut Glass

1876	Telephone introduced by Alexander Graham Bell
1876	Queen Victorian crowned as "Empress of India"
1877	Phonograph invented by Edison (tin cylinder)
1880–c.1915	"Art Nouveau" period (see 1896)
1882	Edison lights lower Manhattan with electricity
1887	Invention of the Graphophone (Bell-Tainter) (wax cylinder)
1888	George Eastman invents the box camera
1891	McKinley Tariff, U.S. imports must bear name of country of origin
1891–1921	"Nippon" era
1892	Louis Comfort Tiffany starts making art glass
1893	Columbian Exposition, Chicago World's Fair
1893	First Sears and Roebuck catalogue
1894	Invention of the Gramophone (Berliner-Johnson) (flat disk)
1895	Marconi invents wireless radio
1896	S. Bing, a German art dealer, opens "La Maison de L'Art Nouveau" in Paris
1897	Dresden Exhibition
1898	Spanish-American War
c.1899	Elbert Hubbard opens Roycroft Guild in upstate New York

Some Interesting 20th Century Dates:

1900	Paris Exhibition
1901	Victor Talking Machine Co. ("Nipper" hears "His Master's Voice")
1901–c.1910	Edwardian Era
1902	Louis Comfort Tiffany takes over family jewelry store in New York City
1904	Louisiana Purchase Exposition, St. Louis World's Fair
1907	"Bakelite" plastic developed by John Baekland
1910	Cylinders discontinued on phonographs, all flat disks
1914	Panama Canal opens
1914–1918	World War I (America enters in 1917)
1915	Johnny Gruelle patents the Raggedy Ann doll
1919	Czecho-slovakia formed (originally hyphenated)
1919–1933	The Bauhaus School, Germany, Walter Gropius
1921	U.S. Tariff act requires imports bear "Made in (country of origin in English)"
1922	King Tut's (Tutankhamen) tomb unearthed by Howard Carter in Thebes, Egypt
1924–1931	Victor Durand makes art glass in Vineland, NJ
1925	Paris "Art Deco" Exhibition
1925	Cranks disappear on phonographs
1926	First television demonstrated by the Englishman, J. L. Baird

1929	Stock market crash in New York begins Great Depression in U.S. (ends ca. 1939)
1933	Chicago "Century of Progress" Exhibition
1934	Charles Darrow creates "Monopoly" game; sells to Parker Bothers in 1935
1936	Homer Laughlin introduces "Fiesta" dinnerware
1938	Roycroft Guild closes
1939	New York World's Fair
1939–1945	World War II (America enters in Dec., 1941, when Pearl Harbor is bombed)
1945–1952	American troops occupy Japan
1945–1965	Mid-Century High Style

Suggested Reading

Advertising Character Collectibles, Warren Dotz (Collector Books).

The Arcanum, Janet Gleeson (Warner).

Bergesen's British Ceramics, Victoria Bergesen (Barrie & Jenkens)

Bessie Pease Gutman: Over Fifty Years of Publication Art, Karen Choppa (Schiffer).

Blue Willow, Mary Frank Gaston (Collector Books).

Cameos, Monica Lynn Clements & Patricia Rosser Clements (Schiffer).

Collectible Souvenir Spoons, Wayne Badersh (Collector Books).

Collecting and Restoring Wicker Furniture, Richard Saunders (Crown).

Collector's Encyclopedia of Depression Glass, Gene Florence (Collector Books).

Collector's Encyclopedia of Limoges China, Mary Frank Gaston (Collector Books).

Collector's Encyclopedia of Noritake, Joyce Van Patten (Collector Books).

Collector's Encyclopedia of Weller Pottery, Sharon & Bob Huxford (Collector Books).

Dog Antiques and Collectibles, Patricia Robak (Schiffer).

Early American Pattern Glass: 1850-1910, Bill Jenks & Jerry Luna (Collector Books).

Fifties Glass, Leslie Pina (Schiffer).

Fifty Years of Collectible Fashion Jewelry: 1925-1975, Lillian Baker (Collector Books).

The Foremost Guide to Uncle Sam Collectibles, Gerald E. Czulewicz, (Collector Books).

The Gem Kingdom, Paul E. Desautels (Random House).

The Glass Gaffers of New Jersey, Adeline Pepper (Scribners).

Hatpins and Hatpin Holders, Lillian Baker (Collector Books).

Hints on Household Taste, Charles L. Eastlake (Dover)

Identifying American Brilliant Cut Glass, Bill & Louis Huxford (Schiffer).

Jugs, a Collector's Guide, James Paton (Souvenir Press).

Maxfield Parrish, Erwin Flack (Collectors Press).

Perfume, Cologne & Scent Bottles, Jacquelyn Jones North (Schiffer).

Pickard China, Alan B. Reed (Collector Books).

The Raggedy Ann & Andy Family Album, Susan Garrison (Schiffer)

Rediscovering Art Deco USA, Barbara Capitman (Viking).

Romantic Staffordshire Ceramics, Jeffery B. Snyder (Schiffer).

Smoking Collectibles, Neil Wood (L-W Book Sales).

Warman's Jewelry, Christie Romero (Warman).

Warwick China, John Rader (Schiffer).

Wave Crest: The Glass of C.F. Monroe, Wilfred R. Cohen (Collector Books).

Wedgwood, Geoffrey Wills (Chartwell).

The World of Edwardiana, Phillipe Garner (Hamlyn).

About The Author

Arthur Schwerdt is an avid antiquer, who one day felt he had accumulated enough to put an "open" sign in front of his house. An antique dealer for over twenty-five years, he has always enjoyed the research as much as the hunt, and frequently shares this research in lectures to collectors' groups and historical societies a well as in seminars, appraisal sessions, and on radio and television. He has been certified as a senior professional appraiser by the National Association of Professional Appraisers and is a member of the New England Appraiser Association. He began writing his weekly column on antiques in 1985. It currently appears in the *Cape May County Herald* newspapers and can be accessed on the Internet at www.capemaycountyherald.com.

The Antique Story Book
is a publication of
The August Farmhouse LLC
since 1983
Antique Furnishings, Decorative Arts and Collectibles
1759 Route 9 North, Swainton, New Jersey 08210
609-465-5135
Garden State Parkway, Exit 13 (Swainton/Avalon)
Member: Cape May County Chamber of Commerce
Avalon Chamber of Commerce

978-0-595-42479-5
0-595-42479-1

CPSIA information can be obtained
at www.ICGtesting.com
Printed in the USA
FFOW04n1113200516
24249FF